CROSSING the LINE OF DUTY

NEIL ROOT

CROSSING the LINE OF DUTY

How Corruption, Greed and Sleaze Brought Down the FLYING SQUAD

First published 2019

The History Press
The Mill, Brimscombe Port
Stroud, Gloucestershire, GL5 2QG
www.thehistorypress.co.uk

British Library Cataloguing in Publication Data.
A catalogue record for this book is available from the British Library.

ISBN 978 0 7509 8920 6

Typesetting and origination by The History Press
Printed in Great Britain by TJ International Ltd, Padstow, Cornwall

CONTENTS

INTRODUCTION

The most routinely corrupt organisation in London.
Robert Mark, Commissioner 1972–77, on the Metropolitan Police CID when
he took over

He was a past master of the arts of falsifying or manipulating alibi statements, the manipulation of identification procedures, and the repeated harassment of witnesses until we had got what we wanted from them.
A former police colleague on ex-Commander Kenneth Drury, Head of the
Flying Squad, The Guardian, *1 August 2003*

More could be added to ex-Commander Kenneth Drury's list of corrupt practices too: taking huge payments and accepting lavish hospitality from a serious criminal; smoothing out a feud between two serious criminals for payment; framing three innocent men for murder, two of whom became broken men after serving eleven years of life sentences; and sharing in the reward money received for those unsafe convictions.

The Flying Squad, also known as the Sweeney, had become a byword for toughness and integrity, and internationally famous. When it began as an experimental mobile police force in 1919 it could never have been known that a man such as Drury would lead it one day. Nor that he would be convicted for corruption, along with a subordinate officer. Neither did the Metropolitan Police ever foresee that the head of the Obscene Publications Squad (aka the Dirty Squad), Det. Chief Supt 'Wicked Bill' Moody, would go to prison too, together with many other officers of that unit. Nor that ex-Commander Harold 'Wally' Virgo, who had authority over nine elite Squads, would be appearing at the Old Bailey, but not for the prosecution. Where's Wally, a wag might have asked. He's in the dock, another could have replied.

It is said that absolute power corrupts absolutely. The independence, autonomy and sheer power wielded by the senior officers of these Squads, along with the trials in the Drugs Squad, and the allegations made against the Fraud Squad, would all be exposed in the 1970s. It is impossible to explore how corruption developed in the Flying Squad without examining the Dirty Squad too. It was a shared culture of ingrained sleaze.

But it had taken decades for the culture which allowed these dishonest officers to wallow in the dirt to develop. This book does not aim to be an exhaustive survey of the Flying Squad's operations from 1919 until it was devolved in the late 1970s. It does follow the work of the Flying Squad and the kind of operations it faced over that period. But it is more concerned with trying to understand how men such as Drury, Moody and Virgo, and other corrupt police officers under them, could have been so corrupt for so long, without their superiors reprimanding or punishing them, and fellow honest officers exposing them.

For the first time, extensive access to the Metropolitan Police Files on the Flying Squad and Dirty Squad investigations from 1972–77, with minimal redaction, allows this book to tell the real story in detail. A Freedom of Information request was also made for the Director of Public Prosecutions files on ex-Commander Drury and ex-Det. Inspector Ingram of the Flying Squad, as these are strangely closed until 1 January 2047. The request was denied, as some persons still living could be affected by their disclosure. The DPP files on the Dirty Squad are already available in the National Archives, the latest released in May 2013, and they have been sourced, although there is little in them not in the Metropolitan Police Files. This is of course because the extensive Metropolitan Police investigations of the 1970s supplied the evidence to the Director of Public Prosecutions to mount prosecutions. So there is probably not much more to be learned from the DPP files on Drury and Ingram of the Flying Squad too.

Other authors, such as James Morton and Duncan Campbell, have done sterling work on this topic before, and their work has been sourced here, alongside others. This author hopes that he has added to their efforts. It is also the first time that a detailed account of Drury's corruption in the Luton Post Office Murder case of 1969, where he framed those three innocent men, has been included in a book along with his Soho criminality. The Metropolitan Police files have also brought new revelations about the Luton case. In the following chapters, Drury's career is traced from 1946 until his death. The incubus and growth of his arrogance, audacity, lack of morality, and the increasing power that fed it, is documented. The corruption within Drury, as with other corrupt senior officers, had become so entrenched over many years that he felt untouchable. When caught, he had no choice but to brazen it out, using the age-old police excuse, 'I was just cultivating an informant', as a fig leaf.

Much has been made of so-called 'Noble Cause Corruption'. This is when a police officer makes a mistake, or cuts procedural corners, to secure the conviction of a suspect he or she thinks is guilty. Such cases obviously do exist, but there is not an iota of nobility in the corrupt practices covered in this book. Greed, ambition and power, and the fact that they could get away with it for a long time and were operating in a climate that made them believe that, are the keys to unlocking the causes here. If someone had asked one of these corrupt officers why they were corrupt, they might have answered, had they chosen to do so honestly, 'because I can be'.

Dick Kirby, an ex-member of the Flying Squad, has published his own history of the Sweeney, but whilst it is good on operational details over the decades, it is very light on the subject of corruption. It is especially kind to ex-Commander Drury. In fact, it was a newspaper article that Kirby published in the *Sunday Express* on 17 July 2011 which motivated this author to write this book. Kirby wrote:

When Ken Drury, the former commander of the Flying Squad was jailed for eight years for corruptly receiving some gold cufflinks and a free holiday in Cyprus in the mid-seventies, the moralists had a field day. The cufflinks and holiday all look like very small beer indeed now.

CROSSING THE LINE OF DUTY

Moralists? Small beer? This book will show exactly what Drury was convicted of, and much else for which he was not, the gravity of some of which is truly appalling. The details of Drury's relationship with the violent and manipulative Soho pornographer James 'Jimmy' Humphreys are also breathtaking at times. This author, like the police officers who investigated Drury in the 1970s, found himself believing Jimmy Humphreys, a seriously nasty man by all accounts, rather than the word of the former Head of the Flying Squad. As a serving Metropolitan Police officer told this author, there was 'barely a cigarette paper between them'.

The late Sir Ludovic Kennedy's seminal 1980 book *Wicked Beyond Belief* about the Luton Post Office Murder case got the two remaining imprisoned men whom Drury had framed, David Cooper and Michael McMahon, released. But their convictions would not be quashed until 2003, after both of them had sadly died. Sir Ludovic Kennedy deserves the highest praise and respect for his efforts on behalf of Cooper and McMahon, as well as for Timothy Evans and Patrick Meehan, amongst other miscarriage of justice cases he championed. This author hopes that this book will remind some and inform others what Drury did to three men in 1969–70, shortly before he became head of the Flying Squad. Especially as Drury was inexplicably never punished for what he did in the Luton Post Office Murder case.

Some of the corrupt links and meetings between Drury, Moody, Virgo and other members of the Flying and Dirty Squads with criminals such as the pornographer Jimmy Humphreys and Bernie Silver of the Syndicate are farcical. That world was sometimes Ortonesque in flavour, but there was menace too, and violence in the Soho air. Pornographers, ponces, pimps, gangsters, armed robbers, cat burglars, safe crackers, smash and grabbers, getaway drivers, killers and policemen, honest and dishonest, live in these pages, roaming London from 1946 to 1978.

Corruption can only breed if it is allowed to, and that is why the times in which corruption was taking root and then thriving are explained, to provide context. How high did the corruption go? The reader must make their own judgement after reading this book, but at the very least there was a conscious turning of blind eyes at a level higher than Drury, Moody and Virgo.

But there is also Sir Robert Mark, the hero and scourge of Met Police corruption. Sadly, as this book will show with the fiasco of Operation Countryman post-Mark, he managed to cut out the culprits, but not the culture of closing ranks.

The legendary TV series *The Sweeney*, plus two film spinoffs, made and first broadcast when these scandals were being exposed, is the public perception of the Flying Squad shared by many. An ex-detective inspector of the Met, who started his career when all this was happening in the mid 1970s, told this author in an interview that the depiction of the Sweeney by John Thaw, Dennis Waterman and Garfield Morgan in the TV show was 'not far off the mark'. Having read transcripts of the words of Flying Squad officers, especially the way that Drury spoke, it does seem authentic.

> You nail a villain and some ponced-up pinstripe Hampstead barrister screws it up like an old fag packet on a point of procedure, then pops off for a game of squash and a glass of Madeira. He's taking home thirty grand a year and we can just about afford ten days in Eastbourne and a second-hand car. It's wrong, my son.'
>
> *Det. Inspector Jack Regan, played by John Thaw, in* The Sweeney

> If I told my blokes to go to the moon, they'd do it. And if, when they got up there, they couldn't find the moon, they'd fucking well plant one there.
> *Ex-Commander Kenneth Drury, Head of the Flying Squad, 1971-2, at a 1971 dinner given in London in honour of the American astronauts who had landed on the moon in 1969, who were present at the event*

The world of Drury, Moody, Virgo and the other corrupt officers was a very different one, before the Police and Criminal Evidence Act (PACE) of 1984. PACE was made law to make a set of ambiguous laws clearer, laws which dealt with police powers. PACE brought in a single law that firmly stipulated and controlled police powers to stop, search, arrest and detain and interview suspected criminals. Perhaps most importantly, it introduced tape recording of interviews. And as we will see, this would have curtailed Drury and other bent officers like him in some of their dirty habits.

Not that PACE has meant that Metropolitan Police officers have always behaved well since 1984. We all know that this is certainly not the case. But it implemented a standard, and it has made it easier to discipline and prosecute wayward officers, as did the Criminal Justice and Public Order Act of 1994. The most shocking aspect of the corruption in the Flying Squad and Dirty Squad in the 1970s and before, as this book traces, is the systemic nature of that corruption. The 2012 exposure of the huge cover-up by West Yorkshire Police of the true causes of the Hillsborough tragedy, fatal police incompetence in preparation and response, and the blaming of the victims and other football fans, is very troubling. This clearly shows that ingrained and widespread corruption has existed on a large scale since the great trials of 1976–77. As recently as July 2013, it was reported in the *Sunday Times*, in a piece by Michael Gillard and David Leppard, that 'Scotland Yard faces a new corruption scandal over claims that its most sensitive units dealing with informants, intelligence and protected witnesses have been "infiltrated" by corrupt officers in the pay of one of Britain's leading organised crime figures'.

Human nature never ceases to shock in its capacity for immorality. Added to that, the novice, innocent or inexperienced can be intentionally implicated by the corrupt, so that they become enmeshed and tainted. The Metropolitan Police, the Flying Squad and even the Dirty Squad had many honest, brave officers in the period covered here, doing their best in sometimes highly dangerous circumstances. This shouldn't be forgotten. But neither should the wrongdoing of certain officers. This is the story of the fall of the Flying Squad and Dirty Squad, and the corruption, greed and villainy that grew within them.

PROLOGUE

Bow Street Magistrates Court, London
30 March 1976

There he was. In the eyes of some a pig in a poke, to others he was an open sore on the vast backside of the most powerful police force in the country, which was now roasting in the disgusting swill of venal corruption. Ex-Commander Kenneth Drury, aged 55, former head honcho of the Flying Squad, the Sweeney, the Heavy Boys, pinnacle of the CID, la crème de la crème of the Metropolitan Police. Grossly overweight, his expensively overfed stomach protruding over the waistband of his straining trousers, suit hardly containing him. Grey hair swept back, sideburns bristly in the style of Lorne Greene in the hit American TV show *Bonanza*.

Another TV show, *The Sweeney*, had already cemented the image of the Flying Squad in the minds of the public. Its third series was due to begin in September that year. Hard-hitting and uncompromising, it had revolutionised the portrayal of the police on British TV when first aired in 1974. This had followed on from the quaintness of *Dixon of Dock Green* and the slightly more hard-edged *Z Cars*. Hints of corruption were written into the scripts of *The Sweeney*, created by Troy Kennedy Martin. But there was always nobility and a sense of 'doing it for the right reasons' running through the central characters.

Drury was in the dock, facing charges of bribery. Drury's television equivalent wasn't Det. Sgt George Carter played by Dennis Waterman, nor Det. Inspector Jack Regan played by John Thaw. It was Det. Chief Inspector Haskins, the boss of the above-mentioned, played by Garfield Morgan. Haskins was an honest copper, although in one memorable episode he was framed by a gangster, the audience forced to question their own judgement about him until the end of the episode exonerated him. Not that Regan or Carter ever doubted their boss. If only the same could have been said of ex-Commander Drury, head of the real Sweeney. But would anybody at that time in the real Sweeney have raised any concerns anyway?

In July of the following year, 1977, Drury would be sentenced to eight years for corruption, but that was in the future. Today he was in court with eleven other suspended or retired Metropolitan Police officers, including ex-Det. Inspector Alistair Ingram, a suspended detective inspector who would be acquitted so should not be named, and ex-Det. Supt Alfred 'Wicked Bill' Moody, former head of the Obscene Publications Squad (aka the Dirty Squad). The almost equally vile but greedier Moody would get twelve years in 1977, as would ex-Commander Wally Virgo, overall head of all the big squads, Flying, Obscene Publications, Drug, as well as six others. However, Virgo's conviction would later be quashed on appeal, reinstating Drury with the very dubious honour of being the sole highest-ranking police officer ever convicted of corruption in Britain.

Ken Drury had resigned as Commander in charge of the Flying Squad almost four years earlier. This was after his almost unbelievably corrupt links to the top Soho pornographer and club-owner Jimmy Humphreys were exposed by the *People* Sunday newspaper on 27 February 1972. Less than three weeks later, on 17 April 1972, Sir Robert Mark became Commissioner of the Metropolitan Police. Mark's avowed mandate was to clean up that institutionally corrupt organisation, the largest and most powerful police force in Britain. This rooting out of insipidity would lead to Drury being arrested on 28 February 1976, taken from his home with a blanket over his head, the tabloids snapping him, an example of illicit police tip-offs of the media working against their own.

That day at Bow Street Magistrates Court was the latest in Drury's court appearances, waiting for committal to trial, and living on bail.

The path to this day had taken many twists and turns, some almost too incredible to believe.

Now, sweating and breathless, dying for a smoke, Drury was facing the music at last. The No. 1 single in the British music charts that week was *Save Your Kisses for Me* by Brotherhood of Man. But Drury knew that only his wife wanted to kiss him any more and that otherwise he was very much alone. But something happened in court that day which was a clue to the true depths of Drury's evil, something for which Drury would never face punishment. Drury's corruption in this case had ruined the lives of two innocent men, tried to do the same to a third, and had massive repercussions on their families too – something which the writer and campaigner for justice, the late Sir Ludovic Kennedy, would call 'wicked beyond belief'.

A young man, dressed very casually, suddenly stood up and started shouting at Drury in front of the court.

'You know me! You picked up my brother Cooper for the Luton murder!'

There was no reaction from the already red-faced and greasily sweating Drury. The man was referring to David Cooper, one of the men whom Drury had framed for the Luton Post Office murder in 1969, when a sub-postmaster named Reginald Stevens was shot dead by a gang of armed robbers. The dark arts of Drury were used to their full in that case, and that's just one that came to light. Drury's amoral corruption almost definitely went back at least to the early 1950s.

All of the officers in court that day were remanded on bail of £5,000 each, a very considerable sum in 1976. But then none of them had had to survive purely on their police wages in earlier years.

No remorse or show of contrition from Drury, showing the arrogance of only the truly rotten and corrupted. What a fucking turn-up, Drury might've said - the ex-Head of the Flying Squad facing lengthy porridge. Beneath Drury's veneer of nonchalance, the beads-turning to-drips of sweat on his brow perhaps betrayed some fear. The prospect of prison with hardened villains, some of whom he'd put there, some legitimately. They'd have him if they could.

But no shame, no shame at all.

Drury and his fellow bent coppers had forever tarnished the reputation of the Sweeney, something even a TV show couldn't entirely wipe away from public consciousness. But then nobody has ever really known the true depths of corruption fathomed by members of the Flying Squad and other elite Metropolitan Police squads.

1

NEW BREED OF CRIMINAL, NEW BREED OF SQUAD

THE FIRST THIRTY years of the Flying Squad since it was formed in 1919 saw it tackle serious criminals committing a multitude of crimes. But there was a huge surge in violent crime in the decade after the Second World War, largely a result of the desensitisation brought about by the war and the higher prevalence of guns in society. This meant that more criminals were armed or 'tooled up' with firearms. Villains had also enjoyed more latitude during the war, when the focus of the authorities was on defeating Hitler and dealing with brutally incessant bombing raids. This fertile criminal environment died hard. Successive governments in the 1950s would take a hard line in fighting this crime epidemic. Pressure would be kicked down from the Home Secretary to the Commissioner of the Metropolitan Police, to the senior CID ranks, and then the Flying Squad. Consequently, the Flying Squad was busier than ever.

The police work closely together with the judiciary, the Directorate of Public Prosecutions and prosecuting counsel in gaining convictions. If the Establishment, led by the Home Secretary and the Home Office, plays hard-ball, the police have to follow, although sometimes the latter can influence the former, of course. As mentioned at the beginning of this chapter, getting arrests and keeping the clean-up rate high was a real pressure in the 1950s as violent crime abounded, both for the Flying Squad and the Metropolitan Police as a whole.

This culture would breed a need to get the cuffs on somebody, and sometimes the wrong person was punished severely, as we shall shortly see in the case of Michael John Davies. Sometimes, the legal establishment hanged people when they should have received a prison sentence. To understand how the Flying Squad developed in the 1950s, and how it became almost autonomous by the 1960s, it is important to understand the legal culture in which it operated. Particularly as that near-autonomy would prove fertile ground in which corruption could grow.

★ ★ ★

Clapham Common, South London, 2 July 1953, evening

The green expanse of the Common was full of young people enjoying the summer breeze. It wasn't uncommon for gangs of teenagers and men in their early 20s known as 'Teddy Boys', as they dressed in Edwardian-style drape coats, to hang around there, and these included the Elephant Mob, the Brixton Boys and the Plough Boys. That night there were about 200 young people there, both male and female. The bandstand in the centre was in full swing, surrounded by a circular area of tarmac with trees evenly spaced out. On the north side, there was a café and dressing rooms, a drinking fountain, as well as benches.

Four young men sat on two parallel facing benches, two on each bench, their legs stretched out to the opposite bench. They were 17-year-old John Beckley, Fred Chandler, aged 18, and two other friends. They weren't from Clapham. The Plough Boys were, and they were named after a pub in Clapham High Street. It was one of the Plough Boys, Ronald Coleman, aged 15, who pushed through the legs of the young men on the benches. One of those on the benches said to Coleman, 'Why don't you walk round the other way, you flash cunt?' Coleman didn't react, but went back to the other members of the Plough Boys standing nearby, and both sets of youths tried to stare each other out. After a while, Beckley and his friends decided to leave the Common as it was getting heavy, and they got off the benches and made towards the road.

But John Beckley and his three friends were just at the drinking foun-tain when the Plough Boys rushed them, and a fight started. As kicks and punches rained down, a witness heard a member of the Plough Boys say 'Get the knives out!' One of the young men from the benches was stabbed, but all four managed to break away and make it on to a Routemaster bus, travelling on the North Side of Clapham Common. But the Plough Boys were in pursuit, and as the bus was stuck in traffic, they jumped aboard and dragged off John Beckley and Fred Chandler at a bus stop. Chandler was stabbed in the stomach and groin, but miraculously managed to get back on the bus and it pulled away. He would survive. However, John Beckley took the brunt of the fury of the Plough Boys, and although he ran away, they chased him until eventually he was cornered against a wall, and in an act of desperate bravado said to his attackers, 'Go on then, stab me, stab me.' One of them did just that, and Beckley slumped to the pave-ment. The bus had now stopped again when they saw the commotion, and once the Plough Boys had run off, one passenger made a call to the police, and another gave aid and comforted Beckley.

John Beckley had received six stab wounds to the body and one to the face. He was pronounced dead at the hospital at around 10.45 p.m. The post-mortem was carried out by the famous pathologist Dr Donald Teare. The police worked quickly, as they had witnesses, although iden-tification of the killer would prove controversial.

The official file on the case in the National Archives holds a letter from the Director of Public Prosecutions to the Commissioner of the Metropolitan Police dated 3 December 1953, which shows how quickly the police of 'L' Division had worked: 'I should like to express my appreciation of the excellent work done by Det. Supt J.M. Davies. It is clear that he and the other officers working under his direction had little respite in the days after the incident on Clapham Common, and I know that many of the people interviewed were reluctant to help police. The success of the investigation is shown by the fact that, within seventy-two hours, five of the six youths concerned in the fight at the bus-stop had been identified and charged.'

The six members of the Plough Boys who would stand trial were Ronald Coleman, aged 15, who had originally provoked Beckley and his friends on the benches; Terence Power, aged 17, Allan Albert Lawson aged 18, Michael John Davies aged 20, Terence David Woodman aged 16, and John Frederick Allan aged 21. Two of them initially denied being on the Common at all that evening, while two admitted being there, but denied being involved in the fight. Michael John Davies surrendered himself at Clapham Police Station on 5 July 1953, three days after Beckley's murder. He said, 'I was there, but I didn't use any knife.' He admitted using his fists.

The trial of all six for the murder of John Beckley opened on 14 September, and the prosecution was led by Christmas Humphreys, fresh from his success in securing the death penalty on Derek Bentley in 1951, and two years away from getting Ruth Ellis sentenced to death. Humphreys told the court that he could find no evidence on the indictment to convict Allan, Woodman, Lawson or Power for murder, and they were kept in custody and later sentenced. Power, Woodman and Allan were given nine months on three counts of common assault to run concurrently, and Lawson got 6 months on the three counts of common assault to run concurrently. Ronald Coleman and Michael John Davies pleaded not guilty to Beckley's murder. Their trial lasted a week, but the jury was unable to agree a verdict after being out for almost four hours.

Then Humphreys decided that he did not want to put 15 year-old Ronald Coleman on trial for murder again – although he had been the one who started the antagonism on the Common- and a new jury was sworn in by the judge, which formally found Coleman not guilty of murder. Coleman received nine months for common assault, and despite his age, he wasn't sent to borstal, but to an adult prison. That left only 20 year-old Michael John Davies to face the murder charge.

Michael John Davies was a labourer from Clapham. His case file shows that he was in the RAF from April 1951 until 28 April 1953, so he had only been out of the force for just over two months when Beckley was killed on 2 July. In the RAF, Davies had been an Administrative Orderly, and no offences were recorded against him.

The trial of Michael John Davies for John Beckley's murder opened on 19 October 1953. Humphreys again prosecuted, with Maxwell

Turner as his junior counsel. The most damning evidence against Davies was a witness statement. Mary Frayling, a secretary, had been on the top deck of the Routemaster bus, and said that she had seen the youth with the knife, and she identified him as Michael John Davies. But he still vehemently denied either having or using a knife. In his opening address for the prosecution, Humphreys said, 'After hearing the evidence you may have no doubt that Davies was using a knife that night. And if in that concerted attack he was using a knife, and a boy died through being stabbed, then that is all you need to find in order to find him guilty. But I ask you to find that it was his hand that stabbed Beckley so that he died.'

Michael John Davies was sentenced to death on 22 October 1953. There was an appeal heard on 30 November and 1 December, and Humphreys focused again on the witness evidence of Mary Frayling. But a crucial factor was that it was getting dark, and she didn't have a clear view. She said the attacker had a colourful tie, and Davies owned one just like it. Even more crucially, Davies was never put on a formal identity parade, as he had admitted from the beginning being involved in the fight. Frayling had picked Davies out in a pre-trial court hearing. No other evidence linked Davies to the knife. The appeal was dismissed, and Davies remained in the shadow of the gallows. On 15 January 1954, a final appeal was heard in the House of Lords, but was dismissed there too. Petitions were drawn up, and eventually the Home Secretary David Maxwell-Fyfe reprieved Davies, and he was given life imprisonment.

Davies continued to plead his innocence, and Lord Pakenham got involved in his case in 1958. Some of the original Plough Boys involved in the fight with Davies denied that he had used a knife on Beckley, but of course they were then safe. Davies was released from prison on 23 October 1960, after serving seven years. He continued to fight for a pardon, and in 1962–63, the famous justice campaigner Lord Longford, whom we will meet again later, was involved in his case. But in 1966, the Home Secretary of the day, Roy Jenkins, said that he could not intervene in the case, as there was no new evidence.

There was massive newspaper coverage of the murder of John Beckley in 1953, and this undoubtedly put pressure on the police to nail a culprit for the stabbing. As we have seen, the judicial climate in 1953–54 for the trial and appeals of Davies was a harsh one, and with the Establishment Buddhist lackey Christmas Humphreys as prosecutor, and the close-to-sadistic Lord Chief Justice being Rayner Goddard, it is little wonder that somebody had to be convicted. A 17-year-old boy had been killed, but then Davies was almost hanged, even though there were severe doubts that he had wielded the fatal knife.

At Davies's trial, one of the policemen giving evidence against him was Det. Constable Kenneth Drury, whom we met in the Prologue. Under presumably rehearsed questioning from junior prosecution counsel Maxwell Turner, Drury said he had purchased a knife thought to resemble the one used to kill Beckley and checked where they could be bought all over London. Drury described it as 'quite a cheap knife' and that such knives were available to buy in many places not far from Clapham Common. In fact, the actual murder weapon was never found.

The police investigation into John Beckley's murder under Det. Supt Davies was run by dividing the officers into two groups: one group took statements and dealt with messages, and the other group was out interviewing people on the streets. The official file shows that Drury was probably in the group taking statements, as his neatly typed and signed statements are still there. Seven police officers, including thirty-two-year-old Det. Constable Drury, were recommended for a commendation on 27 October 1953, five days after Davies was sentenced to death. Drury had last been commended on 4 November 1952, so less than a year earlier. He was a dedicated and fastidious policeman, it would seem.

Kenneth Ronald Drury was born on 18 October 1921. He had been a Post Office messenger boy before joining the Territorial Army in May 1938, aged 16. He was mobilised in October 1939, and served in the Corps of Military Police during the Second World War, reaching the rank of staff sergeant, before being demobilised on 7 June 1946. Just ten days later he joined the Metropolitan Police, Warrant No. 128818.

In his memoirs, the Great Train Robber Bruce Reynolds recalled meeting Drury in 1948 or 1949, when Reynolds was still a teenager and Drury had been in the Metropolitan Police for just two or three years.

Drury's service record in the Metropolitan Police files shows that he had been in uniform in 'A' Division until 12 July 1948, when he joined the CID in 'L' division, which was based in south London, where Reynolds was brought up, and where Drury was still stationed in 1953 when he was involved in the John Beckley murder investigation. So Drury was out of uniform in 1948–49, a plain-clothes Detective Constable, the most junior CID rank.

Already becoming involved in petty crime, Reynolds remembered that he had bought a sunlamp off a friend for £5 *apparently* not realising it was stolen. Next day, Reynolds had a visit at his parents' house from the then 27- or 28-year-old Det. Constable Drury.

'Bought any sunlamps recently?' said Det. Constable Drury.

'Yeah,' said Reynolds.

'Who from?' said Drury.

'A bloke in a pub,' said Reynolds.

Drury fixed Reynolds with a stare for a few moments.

'Are you sure you can't do anything to help me with my enquiries?' said Drury.

Reynolds was nicked, charged with receiving stolen goods and fined £20. The day following Reynolds's appearance in court, Drury turned up again at Reynolds's house. 'Well, you've just paid a twenty quid fine, but I gave you a chance to do something about it. Silly fucker, I could've straightened the whole thing out for a tenner,' said Drury. Not exactly 'Evening all,' the catchphrase of the cheerful policeman played by Jack Warner in the popular police television show *Dixon of Dock Green*, which would begin to be broadcast six or seven years later in 1955, and run until 1976, when *The Sweeney* would be all the rage in living rooms.

Corruption was already rife in London policing. Eric Mason, who would be active in London gangland from the 1950s until the 1970s, said that he had paid the police lots of money since he started out as a criminal, to get bail or to have his previous record shortened for the court before sentencing, as reported by Duncan Campbell in *The Underworld*. When he was detained in Cardiff over a bank robbery, the Welsh policemen made comments about London policemen, 'and how they could afford 500-guinea suits and double-Scotches'. Mason would later be a member of the

Kray firm, and in the mid 1960s received 370 stitches and multiple skull fractures when hit on the head with a chopper by the notorious 'Mad' Frankie Fraser, then working for the rival Richardson gang.

Incidentally, while doing an eighteen-month stretch in Lewes Prison in Sussex as a young man, Bruce Reynolds met another south London criminal just starting out like him. His name was James 'Jimmy' Humphreys, and by the late 1960s, he would be a major force in Soho vice, and will feature heavily in this story later on. More interestingly, the Metropolitan Police files show that while DC Drury was based at 'L' Division in south London, on 19 September 1951, he pulled Humphreys' criminal record file out of the Met's file system, 'to assist him in a case of robbery'. The robbery had taken place in Clapham on 6 September that year, and Humphreys was not arrested after Drury read his file. Twenty years later, Drury and Humphreys would enjoy a lucrative and mutually corrupt friendship, before it turned sour and Humphreys would become Drury's nemesis.

Almost two and a half years after the John Beckley murder investigation, on 28 December 1955, Drury joined C.O.C8, the Flying Squad, where he would stay for a year, until 3 December 1956. On that same day, Drury became a Sergeant (2nd Class). He was rising steadily up the ranks, growing in confidence. The fact that he was seemingly bent just two or three years into his service, when still the lowest rank of detective, tells a troubling story, and also gives a snapshot of how corrupt some members of the Metropolitan Police were in the immediate post-war years, and the climate that allowed it to fester. The police hierarchy was alerted to this corruption. As we shall see, in 1955 Det. Supt Hannam made a report about corruption, focusing on the seminal West End Central police station. But the then Commissioner of the Metropolitan Police, Sir John Nott-Bower, personally went down to West End Central and gave the officers stationed there a pep talk, assuring them that he believed the allegations to be untrue.

Drury's altercation with Reynolds was minor corruption, but from a compromised acorn would grow a rotten tree. By the time that Drury returned to the Flying Squad in 1970, he would be a Det. Chief Supt, brazenly arrogant and deviously cunning.

★ ★ ★

London gangland in the late 1940s up until the mid 1950s was dominated by a power struggle between Billy Hill and Jack 'Spot' Comer.
The Flying Squad had had dealings with both men, Hill since the late
1930s and Comer with the botched Heathrow Bullion Robbery of
1948. Hill especially would continue to be in the sights of the Flying
Squad for the first half of the 1950s, until his semi-retirement in late
1955, early 1956. Comer's influence was waning by the mid 1950s,
and Hill was the dominant force when he stepped back and lived
in Marbella for a time, his empire being run by trusted associates
in London.

But both men would have a major influence on the new force
emerging after 1954 – the Kray Twins (Ronnie and Reggie), and their
'Firm'. The Krays' empire began in Bethnal Green, Mile End, Bow and
Whitechapel in the East End of London and then moved into the West
End, including Soho, in the 1960s. The Richardson gang too, based
around the brothers Charlie and Eddie, whose base was Camberwell
in southeast London, was on the rise. The Krays and the Richardsons
would be the major forces in London organised crime from the late
1950s until the arrest of the Richardsons and their gang in 1966, and the
taking in of the Krays and the Firm in 1968.

The convoluted intricacies of the activities of the Krays and the
Richardsons need not concern us here. The history of both gangs has
been minutely documented and the stories told many times, and the
fact is that neither gang had much involvement with the Flying Squad.
The Krays were involved in armed robbery to an extent, which was still
the main target of the Flying Squad, but there are no recorded alterca-
tions between them. The Krays specialised in extortion and protection
exerted by intimidation, and clubs, while the Richardsons focused on
long firm frauds, scams, fruit machines, extortion by intimidation, and
even had mining and property interests in South Africa for a time. Both
gangs became increasingly violent as they became more powerful, and
the Metropolitan Police, realising the true menace of their spreading
tentacles, set up special investigation teams to bring down both.

However, there is no doubt that both the Krays and the Richardsons would have had corrupt coppers in their pockets. No criminal operation of the size that both gangs built up could have operated without some help from those inclined to use their uniform or rank to make some extra. In fact, Charlie Richardson, no stranger to the protection rackets himself, once said that 'the most lucrative, powerful and extensive protection racket ever to exist was administered by the Metropolitan Police.' He was speaking from personal experience, and whilst both gangs are not major threads in this story, it is important to remember that the Krays and the Richardsons were operating throughout the period covered in this chapter, and that wider Metropolitan Police corruption was taking place while the Flying Squad was occupied with individual armed robberies and the Great Train Robbers. Meanwhile, the Syndicate was simultaneously growing in Soho, preparing the seedy soil in which the corruption that would bring down the Flying Squad and the Obscene Publications Squad in the 1970s could be fertilised.

★ ★ ★

As the 1960s progressed, corruption was both witnessed and indulged in by honest coppers and dishonest police officers and criminals respectively. Michael Hames was an honest policeman, who joined the Met as a probationer and became a police constable in 1964. He would rise to the rank of detective superintendent and become head of the Obscene Publications Branch aka 'the Dirty Squad' in the 1980s and early 1990s, long after the corruption scandal that hit the Dirty Squad in the 1970s.

In his memoirs, Hames recalled how he had brushed up against a corrupt superior whilst a probationer at Albany Street police station, working in shifts of 6 a.m.–2 p.m., 2 p.m.–10 p.m. and 10 p.m.–6 a.m., six weeks on days and three weeks on nights on rotation. On one shift Hames had stopped a club owner of Greek origin, Vasos Avramides, known as 'Petaros', in his car, as he was disqualified from driving. Petaros owned a club in Drummond Street, which is close to Euston Station. The club was frequented by small-time crooks and prostitutes, and so both it and Petaros were very much on police radar. After Petaros had been entered in the charge book, the next day Hames had a visit from a Crime Squad officer at the police station.

The officer explained that another colleague had asked him to speak to Hames on his behalf, and said, 'He says Petaros is a good informant. He wonders if you could forget it.' This shocked probationer Hames, and he didn't agree to anything. The following day, the officer who had sent the previous day's visitor on an errand came to see Hames. He said that it would be 'worth your while' to Hames, if he dropped the charge. Hames asked what that meant, and the officer said 'a hundred quid'. When Hames asked the officer what he himself would get out of it, the officer replied, 'I'll be all right.' Again, Hames didn't commit to anything, and went to see his detective superintendent, who went ahead with the prosecution of Petaros. But when Hames went to see Petaros at his club to serve him with his court summons papers Petaros offered him money and then jewellery, for his girlfriend, as a bribe.

Petaros went on to be fined £50 for driving while disqualified, £10 for driving with no insurance, and he was disqualified for another six months. The irony here was that it would have cost Petaros much more to have paid off corrupt officers than to pay his fines. If Hames's bung would have been £100, the corrupt officer who approached him would have received at least that, and probably much more for his trouble. So instead of paying £60, he would have been obliged to pay a probable minimum of £200 to get the charge dropped, unless the further six months disqualification from driving was worth at least £140, of course. But this is how police corruption worked in practice. The shield of a criminal being an 'informant' to explain why he should be 'sorted out' is one which senior officers would use to explain their close association with high-level criminals in the corruption trials of the 1970s.

The Dirty Squad itself would be at the centre of corruption in the mid 1970s when Det. Chief Supt 'Wicked Bill' Moody, former Head of the Obscene Publications Squad, would be exposed, as we shall see. But the cynical straight face of police rectitude, hiding a cesspit of professional dishonesty beneath, was very much in place by the late 1960s, and in fact far earlier. As has previously been stated, ingrained systemic corruption doesn't grow overnight, but takes years to form and settle.

In 1967, Moody was a detective inspector, and already in the Obscene Publications Squad. The Dirty Squad was then based at West End Central in Savile Row. Moody led raids on the Victoria & Albert Museum and the Tate Gallery, and confiscated books for sale containing nude pictures. In July of 1967, the Home Secretary Roy Jenkins summoned the Commissioner of the Metropolitan Police, Sir Joseph Simpson, to his office. Jenkins told Simpson in no uncertain terms to stop the Dirty Squad from targeting legitimate publications and to focus on real pornography. That, of course, was mainly to be found in Soho. Within a decade, Moody would be arrested for his corrupt links to Soho pornographers.

★ ★ ★

To understand how the Flying Squad and Dirty Squad became enmeshed in the deep corruption of the 1960s and early 1970s, it is important to trace how the activities of Bernie Silver and Frank Mifsud of the Syndicate developed from the late 1950s and how they gripped Soho like a vice in the 1960s. The police would claim that at their peak, Silver and Mifsud were jointly making £100,000 a week, an absolute fortune in the period 1969-72. We should also trace how James 'Jimmy' Humphreys carved his own space in Soho, and how a feud between Humphreys and Silver got the corrupt Commander Kenneth Drury of the Flying Squad an 'in' with the lucrative fruits of Soho pornography in 1971, as the Flying Squad should have been chasing violent armed criminals, and not schmoozing with Soho pornographers – though they too had a propensity for violence sometimes.

Bernie Silver, who was Jewish and born in Stoke Newington in northeast London, had served in the Second World War in the Parachute Regiment, before being discharged on medical grounds in 1943. He thereafter worked in various jobs, before entering the world of vice in the late 1940s, working as a runner for and learning the ropes from the Messinas, then the top dogs in Soho. In fact, he married a Messina prostitute, Albertine 'French Betty' Falzon, who continued to work, Silver poncing off of her earnings.

The ruthless methods of the Messinas must have become deeply ingrained in Silver, as he would become known as a man not to be trifled with at any cost. Silver was smooth and assured, dapper and always elegantly dressed, in sharp contrast to 'Big Frank' Mifsud, his Maltese partner, who was usually scruffy in appearance, so much so that a visitor to Soho, who didn't know who he was, would never have guessed the power he held as the 1960s unfolded. Mifsud was a traffic policeman in Malta before he moved to London, known as 'Big Frank' as he weighed eighteen stone, and was even more feared than Silver. 'Big Frank' was infamous for ordering serious beatings to those who crossed him.

By the early 1950s, Silver controlled clubs in the East End, around Brick Lane. His first known arrest was in 1956, the year of Tommy Smithson's murder, when he was taken in for living off immoral earnings. This involved renting out rooms to prostitutes at vastly inflated rents, with the rent books being doctored to show only about 10 per cent of the rent actually being paid. Silver was becoming heavily involved in property, known as a 'flat farmer', and as we shall see, the ability to get properties cheaply was a necessity to do well in Soho vice. Just as the notorious slum landlord Peter Rachman was doing with his property empire in west London, the manipulation of leasehold properties with 'nominees' or frontmen was imperative. In fact, Rachman also ran a very profitable high-class nightclub called the El Condor in Wardour Street, Soho, for a couple of years in the late 1950s, where Princess Margaret was known to visit.

Racism was also a major problem within the Met at this time, and this would sadly be echoed decades later in the 1990s, in the way that the murder of the black teenager Stephen Lawrence was handled. In her 1979 book *Rachman*, Shirley Green describes one of Rachman's henchmen, an enormously physically strong Austrian ex-professional wrestler named Fred Rondel – he had retired as nobody on the wrestling circuit would risk fighting him, apparently. Rondel, who had suffered brain damage in a Nazi concentration camp, physically evicted a West Indian pimp from one of Rachman's Notting Hill properties in the late 1950s. During the fight, Rondel ripped the pimp's hand in half, bit his ear off and levered his eye out with a thumb. In an example of the racism which would soon lead to the Notting Hill race riots, Rondel remembered that he was given a friendly reception at the local police station, and that the police had a collection for his bail: 'I was out in about ten minutes on £10 bail.' Rondel would go on to receive a three-year prison sentence for grievous bodily harm.

The Messinas, a Maltese gang, had ruled Soho and prostitution in the late 1940s and 1950s, until they were smashed by the media, namely the legendary crime journalist Tommy 'Duncan' Webb, who ran a major exposé of their activities in the *Sunday People*, a newspaper which would play a major part in exposing corruption in the Flying Squad in the early 1970s. Seeing the vacuum left by the end of the Messinas as a dominant force in Soho, Silver hooked up with Mifsud in 1964-65, and they began to buy up property, often using third parties to sign leases or freeholds. In this way, they were not directly connected to their strip-tease clubs and dirty bookshops on paper. But if anyone tried to muscle in on them, they would be taught a lesson.

Starting with the Gigi striptease club in Brewer Street, later relocated on Frith Street, Silver and Mifsud began to spread out in Soho. The Pigalle and the Red Mill were two of many prominent clubs that followed. By the late 1960s, Silver and Mifsud had nineteen Soho clubs, but also massive influence so that anyone moving into Soho would have to pay them something, and by then, also some corrupt policemen indirectly. In fact, it would later come out that various vice operators in Soho had been paying off bent police officers since the early fifties, and the going rate of bribes increased markedly over time. The Syndicate was indeed aptly named, and those working close to Silver and Mifsud included Emmanuel Bartolo, Joseph Mifsud, Emmanuel Coleiro, Frank Melito and Victor Micallef, to name just the most senior in the firm. Silver's HQ was in Romilly Street in an estate agent's office – he called himself an 'estate agent and art dealer' – and later in a bookmaker's in Haymarket.

Another player who would centrally figure in the corruption trials of the 1970s, particularly in relation to the Flying Squad, was James 'Jimmy' Humphreys. Humphreys' criminal record file had been pulled by Kenneth Drury in 1951, and he had made a complaint against 'Tanky' Challenor for corruption in 1963.

Born in Bermondsey in South London on 5 January 1930, Humphreys left school at the age of fourteen, and while still in his teens became friendly with the notorious gangland figure 'Mad' Frankie Fraser. But later events would change this feeling of friendship. In a telephone conversation with David Fraser, Frankie's son, in late 2012, this author asked to interview Frankie about his old friend Jimmy Humphreys. David Fraser said that Humphreys, who died in 2003, had been no friend of Frankie's for many years, and that James Humphreys was 'a grass'. As this book will prove, Humphreys was, with no doubt, a police informer, and in some high-profile cases too.

Humphreys' rap sheet in the Metropolitan Police files is interesting reading and shows how he developed from petty crime as a youngster, before graduating to more serious crime. Just a year after leaving school, 15-year-old Humphreys was arrested for housebreaking and stealing fur coats and other articles, and fined £5 in April 1945 with the end of the war in sight, and seven months later in November, he was committed to Benstead Hall Approved School for 'taking and driving away a motorcar without the owner's consent'. Released on license from Benstead Hall in late August 1946, Humphreys was returned there in October 1947 for receiving a stolen motorcar, clothing, tools, housebreaking and stealing a sewing machine. In June 1948 he was given three years in Borstal for stealing a roll of cloth, and again for taking a motorcar without consent, being released early in February 1950. In November 1950, he was sentenced to his first adult prison term of twelve months, now aged 20, for 'assisting and comforting' two others who had stolen goods worth £22 4s 6d. He was released in June 1951. This is the period in which then DC Kenneth Drury of 'L' Division pulled out his file.

Then in October 1952, it got more serious, and Humphreys got twenty-one months at the Central Criminal Court for receiving a quantity of stolen goods and assault with intent to resist arrest. Coming out in December 1953, he was given a conditional discharge of twelve months in November 1954 for 'loitering with intent to steal from unattended motorcars'. In July 1955, Humphreys broke his conditional discharge order and was arrested for stealing clothing and drapery from a motor van and loitering with intent, receiving two years and three months, from which he was released in February 1957. Then in March 1958 at Glamorgan Assizes, now aged 28, Humphreys got six years for office-breaking and stealing money and postal orders valued at £8,260, two years for conspiracy to dispose of a postal order, and three months for receiving a stolen driving licence, forcing the rear door of a sub-post office using bodily pressure, and using explosives to open a safe.

When Jimmy Humphreys was released on 26 October 1962, he was 32 years old. Handsome and desperate to 'make it', he had already been married once, to a woman called June Driscoll. After serving four and a half years in Dartmoor Prison, it is little wonder that he decided to find another way of making money. Humphreys hooked up with an old girlfriend from the early 1950s again in Soho, Rusty Gaynor (real name June Gaynor), a former barmaid and ex-model, now a stripper, whom he would marry in May 1963. Humphreys took a lease on premises in Old Compton Street, Soho, and it was soon thriving, with various 'faces' frequenting it.

Many have said that Rusty had a good business brain, and this undoubtedly helped Humphreys. Humphreys had to pay 'protection' to a corrupt policeman Det. Sgt 'Tanky' Challenor, later convicted and then certified insane. Challenor told Humphreys to move his club to Macclesfield Street, which he did. But once in new premises, Challenor reappeared and asked for more money, and Humphreys paid another £50 in total. It was then that Humphreys made a complaint to Scotland Yard, which was disbelieved, but which we now know was almost definitely true. Humphreys must have felt some satisfaction when Challenor went down.

The Macclesfield Street club thrived, and soon Humphreys was looking for other premises to lease. His string of striptease clubs and pornographic bookshops would spring out from Walker's Court off Brewer Street, starting at No. 5. It was called the Queen's Club, and it was very lucrative immediately, allowing Jimmy and Rusty to buy a large farmhouse called Frogs Hill House, in Newendon, Kent. Later the Queen's would relocate to the corner of Berwick Street, where it would do even better. It became decidedly upmarket for Soho, with the old Walker's Court premises operating as a booking office for the new Queen's.

One of the dancers choreographed by Rusty at the Queen's was Mary 'Norma' Russell, who would later become Norma Levy, and bring down Lord Lambton, the Conservative Minister in charge of the RAF, in a prostitution/marijuana scandal in 1973. After his resignation from the government, Lambton said, 'I like to believe there's a little foolishness in every man.' Despite his growing success, Humphreys was always weary of Silver and Mifsud and the Syndicate, as anybody operating in Soho at the time necessarily was if they wanted to survive. However, one of Silver's bookshops was also in Walker's Court. The outwardly good-mannered Jimmy Humphreys obviously didn't upset Silver, or he would have been forced out.

But we will see that Humphreys was actually a hardened and ruthless man himself, preying on less well-connected operators. Not that he could even attempt to show that side of himself when dealing with Silver or Mifsud- they were just too powerful. Some have said that Silver was 'grooming' Humphreys as his successor, but this is very doubtful. They tolerated each other, perhaps became friendly for a time. Silver obviously saw that Humphreys and his wife could make him money, which they would from 1969. Humphreys needed Silver to progress, as he was only bottom to midway in the Soho food chain in the early–mid 1960s. Later, he would have real power too, especially due to his corrupt links to senior police officers, but never to the extent of the Syndicate.

Jimmy and Rusty Humphreys were now enjoying a luxurious lifestyle- an apartment in Ibiza and a flat in Dean Street, Soho, were added to Frogs Hill House in their property portfolio. Humphreys even became Chairman of Hastings United, a small football club in Sussex, not so far from Frogs Hill House. But when other directors found out about his serious criminal record, he was forced out, and Frogs Hill House was sold soon after. The Dean Street flat in London was now the centre of the Humphreys' lives, and Humphreys could be seen driving around in a Rolls Royce, later a Jensen, and eating at the SQPR restaurant in Dean Street. They were making serious amounts of money, and this would only increase as the 1960s gave way to the 1970s.

But Humphreys did have his troubles in the sixties. In 1964, one of his clubs was firebombed. It was thought to be the Richardson gang trying to muscle in on Soho, but never proved. Humphreys put up steel shutters, a feature that would become normal practice for clubs and bookshops as time went on, acting as a guard against attacks when premises were closed. Even Silver and Mifsud would have problems in late 1966 and early 1967, when two of their striptease clubs – the Gigi (Frith Street) and the Keyhole (Old Compton Street) – were firebombed, along with a gambling club they owned in Greek Street. It wasn't long before Tony Cauci, a part owner of the Carnival club with Mifsud, was arrested, along with Cauci's underling Derek Galea. Cauci had taken umbrage as he felt that he should have a bigger ownership share of the Carnival. The Carnival wasn't targeted, of course. Galea would give evidence for the prosecution against Cauci in the end, influenced by Mifsud. Cauci and Galea, both Maltese, got serious sentences in a retrial, as the first trial was found unsafe as a witness had committed perjury.

The year 1966 was also an eventful one for Humphreys. He appeared at Bow Street Magistrates Court in July according to the Met files, facing three charges. They were his first convictions since 1958, but very minor when compared to robbery with explosives. The charges were for 'unlicensed public music and dancing (striptease)' in his clubs on three occasions that year, twice in January and once in February. For each charge, there was a fine or term of imprisonment alternatively: In January, £100 and £150 to be paid in seven days, or one months' and two months' imprisonment respectively; in February, £200 to be paid in seven days or three months' imprisonment. There is little doubt that Humphreys wouldn't have needed seven days to pay the £450 owed in total.

That year, when England won the football World Cup at Wembley, was also when Jimmy and Rusty formed their company, Humphreys Entertainments Ltd. The Met files show that on 19 August 1966, a hundred £1 shares were issued in the company, and that the registered office was 70 New Cavendish Street, London W1. The directors were Jimmy, who had one share, Rusty with sixty-four shares, William Beaton with one share, Nora Staiano, whose namesake Raphael Staiano had one share, and two relatives of Jimmy, both who shared his Christian name: James Sidney Humphreys, and James Louis Humphreys with thirty-three shares, the latter also being the company secretary. There were no mortgages or debentures, and the company and directors were listed as 'Theatre Club proprietors'.

So as the 1960s came towards a close, Silver, Mifsud and Humphreys were gaining in power, and their cultivation of corrupt policemen in the Flying Squad and the Dirty Squad obviously lubricated their progress. In the mid 1970s, Humphreys recalled that Silver once advised him on bribing police officers, and told him to 'Get them when they're young'. In actual fact, the officers who would be exposed as having corrupt associations with Silver, Humphreys and others in the early 1970s would mostly be very senior officers in their forties and fifties. But they were young once, of course, too.

★ ★ ★

The second half of the 1960s and the 1970s was also the period in which armed robbery really came of age, and the numbers of raids on banks, post offices, security vans and wages snatches proliferated. Gangs who used guns or coshes, jemmies or iron bars were seen as of a higher pecking order to other thieves. Safe-blowing was still a respected speciality, and was often still used in raids where a safe had to be breached. Guns especially were becoming more common, with wider accessibility, and in the 1960s housebreakers and burglars would sell any guns they pilfered on to armed robbers, the asking price being between £20 and £30.

There were still Second World War guns in circulation, but shotguns, as used by farmers, were growing in use, frequently with the barrels sawn-off to make them more portable in robberies, for concealment on the approach, and to hasten getaways. This would keep the Flying Squad in work, in more ways than one. But the West End was riddled with police corruption, even on the repressed gay scene, in real-life situations worthy of the black-humoured farce of the plays of Joe Orton. the Serious Crime Squad would eventually bring in Silver and Mifsud of the Syndicate who ran Soho. Very senior officers such as Commander Harold 'Wally' Virgo of Central Office and Det. Chief Supt 'Wicked Bill' Moody of the Dirty Squad were in cahoots with Silver, as well as with Jimmy Humphreys and various other vice operators. Commander Kenneth Drury, soon to be Head of the Flying Squad, would soon join that list of corrupt senior officers linked to Soho too.

2

THE LUTON POST OFFICE MURDER

Barclays Bank car park, Welbeck Road, Luton, Bedfordshire, Wednesday, 10 September 1969, just after 6 p.m.

IT WAS A pleasant late summer evening, and Reginald Stevens, a man of routine, had just locked up the Post Office on High Town Road where he held the position of postmaster. Stevens, aged 51, always parked his blue Sunbeam Rapier in the bank car park, a short walk from work. The car would remain there all day, until he locked up the Post Office at 6 p.m. sharp and then often stopped at the newsagents on the corner, before walking back to his car to drive home. This evening, he bought an evening newspaper first, not knowing that his movements were being watched. Stevens got into his car, and then suddenly, three men walked towards him. Two were younger, around their early 30s: one was very well built and short with blonde hair, the other tall with long sideburns and dark hair. The third was perhaps ten years older, short and fat with dark dishevelled hair. What Stevens didn't know was that one of the men had a hidden shotgun.

Stevens never stood a chance. The idea was obviously to get the Post Office keys off Stevens, hold him until they had plundered the building of everything worth taking, load it on to the false number-plated green van stolen the previous day waiting nearby, behind the wheel of which was a thin, nervous man in his late 40s with grey hair and a washed-out face, get away, and then leave Stevens stranded somewhere in the middle of nowhere, away from Luton. But it didn't work out like that.

All that is known for sure is that the shotgun went off more than once, the bullets going into Stevens's stomach, either because he wouldn't hand over the keys, or just by accident. What is known is that the plan wasn't to shoot him. Stevens was dead within seconds, his blood hitting his killer and the inside of his car. The three men ran from the Sunbeam Rapier and back to the van, engine revving noisily, which sped off down High Town Road, mounting a pavement, and with one of the gang still holding on to the side of the van, almost hit another car, and then made it round to Luton train station car park, where the gang had left two other cars – a red sports car and a Vauxhall – drove over the station footpath, and then stopped.

All four men got out. One man threw a brown holdall bag over onto the railway embankment, and said, 'Well, that's that.' The van driver and the man who had thrown the holdall both got into the Vauxhall, and the other two into the red sports car. Both cars then pulled away, leaving the green van in the station car park. Both cars then drove in the direction of London 40 miles away on the M1 motorway. They hadn't blagged anything, and a man had died.

★ ★ ★

An armed raid of this type would usually have gone straight to the Flying Squad, especially as there had recently been a string of Post Office robberies. But as Stevens had been killed, it went to COC1, and the Murder Squad in the Crime & Operations department. Put in charge of the Reginald Stevens murder investigation, which would swiftly become known as the 'Luton Murder', was our old friend Det. Chief Supt Kenneth Drury.

Drury was now aged 48. After leaving the Flying Squad and moving to 'E' Division on 3 December 1956 as a detective sergeant (2nd class), he had served three months in 'P' Division until 27 April 1957. Then he had transferred back to 'L' Division, where of course he had served for over seven years from 1948 to 1955. While at 'L' Division, he had propositioned a young Bruce Reynolds, pulled out Jimmy Humphreys's criminal file and was part of the John Beckley murder investigation in 1953. On 27 April 1957, he became a detective sergeant (1st class). After almost another six years in 'L', Drury was promoted to detective inspector on 25 February 1963, at the age of 41, transferring to 'M' Division on the same day.

In the next six years, he would rise quickly, and gain wide experience. Drury stayed at 'M' Division only until 3 February 1964, then spending four months with 'R' Division, returning to 'M' until 2 November 1964. Next he joined C.1 (Central Office) until 1 September 1965, when he moved to the Regional Crime Squad (RCS). On 1 April 1966 he became a detective chief inspector, moving to COC1. He was made a detective superintendent there on 1 May 1967, and again promoted to detective chief superintendent on 16 October 1967, moving to 'Z' Division. On 1 May 1968, DCS Drury transferred back to COC1. There he was attached to the Murder Squad when Reginald Stevens was shot dead in a Luton car park on 10 September 1969.

The burly, rotund Drury, fag in mouth, the corrupt reverse of Columbo, was soon on the scene. The fictional television detective Columbo had first appeared in the United States in the TV movie *Prescription Murder* in the previous year and would go on to wow British fans for years. Like the Los Angeles detective in the rumpled mac, Drury would unravel leads to find the killer(s), but unlike the fictional Lieutenant Columbo, Drury wouldn't follow leads and use his cunning to ascertain the facts, but would fit the facts to his leads, and use his cunning to tidy up any inconvenient truths, as we shall see.

The murder of Reginald Stevens attracted enormous publicity, both on television and in the newspapers. The authorities were outraged, and the Post Office immediately offered a substantial £5,000 reward for information that led to the arrests and conviction of the killers. While one man pulled the trigger of the shotgun, under the law of joint enterprise, all four of them, including the getaway driver in the green van, would be culpable, as Derek Bentley unjustly and fatally discovered back in 1952. Capital punishment was abolished in Britain in 1965 by the Murder (Abolition of Death Penalty) Act, and the last executions, two on the same day, had taken place in 1964, in different prisons. Five years later in 1969, the joint enterprise killers of Reginald Stevens therefore wouldn't hang, but they would face life imprisonment, and the wrath of the public, police and prison authorities. It was a nasty, pointless, tragic and shocking crime, even if the gun went off by accident. The problem was that Drury would deliberately ensure that three men were imprisoned for the murder, three men who didn't do it. The one man that Drury found who was definitely involved, the driver of the green getaway van, was allowed to turn Queen's evidence and remain free. But the resourceful Drury did so much more too.

The pressure was on Drury to get a result, as he was working in the shadow of news bulletins and headlines about the murder. He was also a man on a steep upward career trajectory. Could he make commander? He needed arrests, and high-profile ones like this would be plum ones. So, what did Drury have?

Firstly, he knew from experience that this wasn't the work of a local team, but a London firm. Secondly, he had witnesses who had seen the men, both in the train station and Barclays Bank car parks, where the vehicles were left and Reginald Stevens was murdered respectively. It had been a nice evening, still daylight, and people had seen and heard things. Two women, a Mrs Crawley and a Mrs Calvert, heard the shots and the former saw a man running and get in the back of the green van. Mrs Calvert described him as 'lean, perhaps in his teens, dark-haired'. Significantly, as will be revealed later, Mrs Crawley also said, 'I wouldn't recognise him again.'

Most importantly, Herbert Andrews had just arrived by train on his commute back from work in London, and was in the station car park when the green van raced there after the murder. He was walking on the station footpath and saw the four men jump out of the van and gave descriptions of three of them, but not the fourth. Having realised that something wasn't right, especially when he saw the brown holdall being hurled over the fence, he made a note of the number plate of the Vauxhall as it drove off, on the corner of his evening newspaper. He jotted down 5075 MW – it was close, as the real registration turned out to be 5075 MV. He managed to get a letter and two numbers from the red sports car too, and he was far less sure of those, but he did say that the car had a 'hard top'.

The question was whether a professional gang would use their own cars to travel to and from Luton after the job, or were they stolen? Luckily for Drury, the Vauxhall was soon traced to the ownership of Reg Elliott, who lived in Dagenham, east London. But the car wasn't there. It transpired that Reg had been visited by his brother Alfred, 'Alf', who went by the name of Mathews. Mathews had given his brother £37 and told him that he had sold the Vauxhall. The car was later found abandoned in another part of east London, wiped clean of fingerprints. It was also later discovered that Alf Mathews had got his wife to write out a change of ownership card using a fake name and address for a new owner and send it off to the authorities. The new owner had *apparently* bought the car on the day before the murder. This all happened later on the night that Stevens had been killed. After that, Mathews had laid low at a friend's house, before going to Eastbourne in Sussex with his wife. Finally, Mathews went into hiding at the house of his other brother Albert in Ilford, east London. That's why there was no trace of Mathews at his flat, in Clarion House, Roman Road, Mile End in east London. This had been very much the territory of the Krays before they were arrested in the previous year.

Alf Mathews (Elliott) was now in his late 40s, and was basically a 'gelly' man, his speciality being to blow safes with gelignite. But he also acted as a getaway driver, being good behind the wheel. Mathews had lived a life of crime for a long time. Another villain called George Madsden later gave a statement to a lawyer involved in the Luton Post Office Murder, saying that he had been on a job with Mathews and two others in September 1953. The job was in Dorset, and Mathews had blown the safes, so that they got away with £300–400. They had been arrested on the return journey to London, and Madsden had received six years, while Mathews only got six months. This was because Mathews had made a statement saying that he had been paid £10 to act as a driver, and only that. Mathews had also later received five years for the robbery of a hospital. In his interview, George Madsden said of Mathews: 'In my opinion he is a rat, and will do anything to extract himself from trouble.' As we will see, Matthews was far from just the driver on the Luton job too.

Mathews' wife Florrie said that she had no idea where he was, and neither did his brothers. So they all claimed. But a neighbour of Mathews told Drury that she had seen him leave his flat with three other men, of whom she gave good descriptions, on the day of the murder. This was at about 3.30 p.m.. Mathews, who was carrying a holdall, and the fat man, got into the Vauxhall, the tall, dark man with sideburns got into the green van, and the well-built blonde man into the red sports car. They all drove off, no doubt to arrive in Luton in good time for Reginald Stevens to lock up. Another witness, a car-dealer called John McNair, had also seen the van, the driver and the man holding on to the side, in Welbeck Road in Luton, as it screeched away after the murder. McNair was shown photographs of suspects by the police, and he chose one of Alf Mathews as his second choice.

Added to this, when the brown holdall on the embankment was opened, the shotgun was found inside, and it had Stevens' blood on it. This was found to belong to a Michael Good. Then Good's wife Patricia gave a statement to the Luton police on 27 September, seventeen days after the murder, saying that she had given the gun to her brother, Terry Langston, when her husband had gone to prison for armed robbery. But Good was a free man on the day of the murder, and his appearance matched several witness statements of one of the men seen in Luton that day. A lawyer who would be deeply involved in the case throughout the 1970s and beyond, Gareth Peirce, later thought it 'an overwhelming likelihood' that Good himself took part in the crime itself, according to Ludovic Kennedy, who would write a seminal book on the case.

Terry Langston was taken from his home to Luton police station and interviewed by Drury on 30 September 1969. It would later transpire that Mathews picked up the gun from Langston on the morning of Stevens' murder. Langston told Ludovic Kennedy in 1979 about his encounter with Drury: 'It was put to me that I knew what the questioning was about – murder. I was told that I was up to my neck in it, and that I was going to be charged with it.' Langston denied ever 'handling' or using the shotgun.

Drury was unable to locate Alf Mathews, who was still skulking in his brother Albert's home in Ilford. Mathews was by far the strongest suspect in the case. Not to be idle and under pressure, dynamic Drury began to cast his net around for other possible suspects. Mathews had been connected to the Vauxhall, but there was also the red sports car to consider. This car, and investigations already going on into another two recent Post Office robberies, would lead Drury, the future Head of the Flying Squad, to the three men whom he would frame for the murder of Reginald Stevens.

★ ★ ★

Those three men were David Cooper (real name John Disher), aged 27, Michael McMahon, aged 25, and Patrick 'Patsy' Murphy, aged 26. They were all criminals with previous convictions, mostly relatively minor ones. Murphy's father Stephen, or 'Stevie', was also a good friend of the south London gangland figure Joey Pyle, who had come to notice during the Pen Club fight in 1960. In that fight, Selwyn Cooney, who managed a club for Billy Hill in the West End, had been murdered. For being involved in the fight in the club in Spitalfields, east London, Pyle had received an eighteen-month sentence. Pyle will re-emerge in Kenneth Drury's story later.

Cooper (Disher) was a window-cleaner by trade, and had convictions for assault, theft, stealing, office-breaking, and being in receipt of stolen detonators. In the summer of 1968, just over a year before the Luton Post Office Murder, Cooper had been arrested when explosives, a sawn-off shotgun, guns and ammunition were discovered in his car boot. In fact, they were not his, and he had been given them to get rid of by the girlfriend of a friend who had just been arrested and was in custody. The friend's girlfriend backed up his story, and Cooper only got twelve months inside. Cooper also owned a red Mercedes sports car.

McMahon was a painter and decorator, and had previous convictions for being in possession of an offensive weapon, obtaining by deception, stealing, housebreaking, conspiracy to rob and driving while disqualified. Unlike Cooper, he had a girlfriend, Susan, whom he would marry and who would stand by him throughout all his future troubles and traumas. Murphy was an upholsterer, and had previous for assaulting a policeman, stealing and receiving, housebreaking, and dangerous driving. He was married with a daughter, but was now separated from his wife and had a girlfriend, whom he was planning to marry in January 1970. He owned a red Triumph sports car.

David Cooper knew Alf Mathews, and had carried out several robberies with him, only one of which was successful, and no violence had been used. Cooper had visited Mathews at his flat in Roman Road several times, and Mathews had also spoken to him on Cooper's doorstep a few times, the latter occasions being in the first months of 1969. McMahon and Murphy had never met Mathews. McMahon did know Michael Good slightly, the original owner of the shotgun that had killed Reginald Stevens, but apparently considered him crazy and tried to avoid him when possible.

All three men had been involved in police investigations into Post Office robberies during the summer of 1969, a couple of months before the Luton Post Office Murder. Specifically, two robberies in east London had enmeshed them in police enquiries. One had taken place in Newington Green Road in Dalston Kingsland on 20 May 1969, and another in Middleton Road near London Fields on 7 July 1969. Two days after the latter robbery, Michael McMahon was at his flat in Leytonstone, with his girlfriend Susan and his friend David Cooper, who would soon feel the heat too, and one of Cooper's completely straight brothers. McMahon had been told by his mother and another friend earlier that day that the police were looking for him, and he had phoned Wood Green police station as requested. But McMahon was told that the officer dealing with the matter wasn't at the station at that time. That's why the next events were such a shock to him.

It was at about 9.30 p.m. that same evening that the police surrounded McMahon's flat – it is not recorded whether it was the Flying Squad, but it probably was, as the officers were armed. Susan opened the door, and the police officers ran in heavily. One officer pointed a gun at McMahon and shouted:, 'If you so much as move an inch, I'll blow your fucking head off!'

Cooper and his brother were cuffed together, and McMahon was frogmarched into the bathroom, where he said the police began to use 'heavy tactics', demanding to know the location of 'the lock-up garage'. The police never said that he was a suspect in the Middleton Road Post Office robbery. McMahon's bewilderment only made his fear deeper. Eventually, McMahon was taken to Wood Green police station as he had stolen furniture in his flat. After the police searched Cooper's flat and discovered a stolen washing machine, Cooper was soon at the police station too.

They knew that they would be in the cells overnight, until they went up before the Magistrates' Court the next morning. But they asked a detective (so therefore CID) if they would be able to get bail in court. The detective enquired how much Cooper and McMahon would pay him and another officer if they 'supported' their application for bail. A deal was done after negotiation, and both Cooper and McMahon would have to pay £100 each, the money to be given to the officers in a pub the next evening when they'd been released. McMahon remembered later that, 'These kinds of deals between criminals and police were a regular occurrence, and most criminals expected such "expenses" when they discussed the question of bail.'

But before their court appearances the next morning, the detective returned, obviously having made enquiries, and said that Cooper's bail would be supported, and he was duly released on bail. But McMahon's bail could not be engineered, as the Post Office had taken 'an interest' in him. McMahon fitted the description of a member of an armed gang that had been targeting post offices. It would soon transpire that McMahon was a suspect in no less than ten post office robberies. McMahon was given remand for a week in Brixton Prison, which was broken up by his attendance at an ID parade at Wood Green police station, from which he was not picked out. Finally given bail, supported by the bent detective, McMahon paid the £100 a few days later.

Neither Cooper nor McMahon had had any involvement in any post office robbery, and neither had Murphy. But Murphy's red Triumph sports car had been used in the Middleton Road robbery on 7 July 1969. He had also been seen with two men who would be convicted of carrying out that robbery. When the police searched his lodgings, they found more than £300 in cash, which Murphy said had come from his uncle after a car had been sold. But Murphy was arrested for the Middleton Road robbery too. Put on another ID parade at Wood Green police station on 17 July, he was selected by a witness of the Newington Green Road robbery, which had occurred on 20 May. Murphy was charged and bailed.

So Murphy, Cooper and McMahon were all within the orbit of police inquiries regarding other post office robberies in the summer before Reginald Stevens was shot dead in Luton on 10 September. They were all low-level criminals, not armed robbers like the ones who went to Luton and killed a man. None of them had ever used violence, except for assaulting a police officer when trying to get away. But they were all on hand when Det. Chief Supt Drury needed likely lads for the Luton Post Office Murder. Drury may even have seriously suspected them at first. But this is unlikely, as Drury was very experienced and knew the kind of heavy criminal he was after, and these three men were not of that villainous calibre. Besides, all three of them were nowhere near Luton on 10 September 1969. The key times on that day were between 5.30 p.m. and 7 p.m.. Alf Mathews and the Luton gang had had to get to Luton, 40 miles from London, and Reginald Stevens was shot at around 6.06 p.m., with them having to change vehicles and drive back to London.

Patrick 'Patsy' Murphy rose late that day, and a friend, who was on bail for the Middleton Road robbery, came round to borrow his Triumph again. This seems risky of Murphy in hindsight, as the car had been used in that robbery. When the friend returned with the car, Murphy, the friend and another mate watched the horseracing on TV. Murphy then drove his Triumph further east in London to Ilford (coincidentally where Alf Mathews would hole up with his brother soon after) at 4.30 p.m., to see his father. Murphy was seen in his car by a family friend, but Murphy was distracted, so there was no acknowledgement between them. Arriving at his father's house just after 5 p.m. to find his father out, he waited. When his stepmother and father came home they all had some dinner together, and then a plumber arrived at about 6 p.m.

to do some work. At 7.30 p.m., Murphy drove back to his lodgings and later went shopping with his girlfriend.

Michael McMahon was actually in court on the day of the Luton Post Office murder, arriving at Thames Magistrates' Court with his father and a friend at 2 p.m. McMahon was facing another charge of receiving stolen goods for which he had been caught in August. After being bailed, McMahon saw his friend David Cooper, who had come to the court to support him. Cooper offered all three of them a lift home in his red Mercedes. After Cooper had dropped them off, McMahon stayed at home and watched horseracing – it was the day of the St Leger. At around 5.30 p.m., he went to his girlfriend Susan's flat. When Susan arrived, they had dinner, before going out to a pub at 9.30 p.m..

After Cooper left the home of the McMahon's after dropping them off with their friend, he drove his red Mercedes to the same building where Murphy lived. Although Cooper wasn't there to see Murphy, but another friend who owed him some money. After that, at about 4 p.m., Cooper called his lawyer to talk to her about his court appearance for the next day. This was regarding the stolen washing-machine, for which he would be given a six month suspended sentence later in September. Cooper then drove to his tailor, who would well remember Cooper being there well, and he had a fitting for a new suit. Following that, Cooper got home at about 5.30 p.m., and his brother was there. At around 6 p.m., a friend came round, arranging to borrow the red Mercedes at a later date. At 6.30 p.m., Cooper and his brother went to a pub in Hackney, but were stood up by two women they had arranged to meet there. They went to an amusement arcade and then to see if they could find some nurses to chat up near a local hospital. They then went home.

So Murphy, McMahon and Cooper all had alibis for the time in which the Luton Post Office Murder was committed. These alibis came from family, girlfriends, and from a few witnesses who knew them well, or fairly well. But once DCS Drury got his talons into them, this would stand for very little.

★ ★ ★

On 20 September, ten days after the Luton Post Office Murder, Murphy appeared at Tottenham Magistrates' Court to be remanded on the Newington Green Road robbery charge. His father Steven was with him, and later recalled how a policeman, not in uniform, so therefore a detective, came up to him outside the court. The detective told Steven Murphy that his son Patrick was a suspect in the Luton Post Office Murder, as was his friend who had been charged with the 7 July Middleton Road post office robbery. Several days after that, Cooper came home to be told that two CID detectives from the Regional Crime Squad had asked to meet him in a local pub. He went to meet them, and they told him that they were investigating the Luton Post Office Murder. The detectives added that they knew that the team who had killed Reginald Stevens came from east London.

One of the detectives, DC Laver, made a point of mentioning the £5,000 reward on offer from the Post Office. DC Laver suggested that if Cooper had any relevant information, there were 'ways of paying reward money in a very discreet manner'. Cooper said that he knew nothing, and that he wasn't a grass anyway. They then asked him if he still had his Vauxhall car, and he said that he'd sold it. Cooper didn't mention his red Mercedes because he wasn't asked about it, but this would be held against him later. The detectives already knew that a Luton witness, Herbert Andrews, had seen some of the gang get into a red sports car. Shortly after, Cooper decided to sell his Mercedes as he needed cash. The car dealer who was handling the sale for him told him that two plainclothes coppers, whose descriptions fitted DC Laver and his colleague, had been sniffing around the Mercedes and inspecting it closely. The car remained on sale for a while longer, and then Cooper decided that he wanted to keep it.

McMahon was also approached, but outside court, where he was appearing on the handling stolen goods charge. This time, three detectives asked him if he had any information about the Luton Post Office Murder. McMahon too was reminded about the £5,000 reward. McMahon told them that he knew nothing and that 'robbing post offices is not my scene.' But just a few days later, Michael Good, the original owner of the murder weapon, whom McMahon knew but thought dangerous, came to see McMahon. Good told him that he had been at Ponders End police station the night before, and had been questioned by DCS Drury. In the course of the questioning, Drury had mentioned other suspects he believed were involved in the Luton Post Office Murder: McMahon and Cooper, as well as other names. Apparently Drury had said to Good, 'You can tell that lot I'll wrap this case up in the end.' According to Ludovic Kennedy, Good was a police informer, and it is probable that Good was being used as a pawn by Drury to stir things up. Although it would later be thought likely that Good was involved in the crime himself.

Murphy too was understandably stressed when in mid October his friend who had been charged with the Middleton Road post office robbery was also questioned by Drury at Ponders End about the Luton Post Office Murder. Drury told Murphy's friend that both he and Murphy were seen as suspects in the crime. Cooper too had heard on the grapevine that he, McMahon and Murphy were considered suspects in the Luton murder. It wouldn't be long before Drury made his move for them.

★ ★ ★

Luton Police Station, 22 October 1969

Alf Mathews was sitting before Det. Chief Supt Kenneth Drury, telling him what he was doing on the day of the Luton Post Office Murder, 10 September, almost six weeks earlier. Mathews said that on that day he'd been ill in bed with flu and dysentery. At about 5–5.30 p.m., Mathews said that his brother Reg had come over and Mathews gave him £35, having the previous day sold Reg's Vauxhall for £55, but Reg owed him £20 anyway. Matthews explained that a man had bought it off of him, as he had put a 'For Sale' sign on it. The Vauxhall had of course been used in the Luton job. When Drury asked him why the ownership card had been sent to the authorities on the day after the Luton Post Office Murder, when the car had been sold on the day before the murder, Mathews had an answer ready. Of course, Mathews knew more than anyone that the Vauxhall had been used on the Luton job:

Mathews: Oh, after I sold the car, my wife was approached, and a woman said if anyone asks who I sold the car to, I wasn't to remember, otherwise there would be trouble. I was approached too by a man who said if I didn't want to get hurt, I'd better forget who I sold the car to.

When Drury asked Mathews to give a description of the man he had sold the Vauxhall to, Mathews said, 'He was dark. He'd done a lot of sunbathing. Looked as if he'd lived off the fat of the land.'

Drury: I'm putting you up for identity.
Mathews: I wouldn't entertain anything like this. I wouldn't even go with them.
Drury: If you knew it was going to be a murder?
Mathews: I tell you straight, I wouldn't even kill a bird. This isn't my game.
Drury: As far as I am concerned, you were asked to be the driver.
Mathews: No.
Drury: I am going to put you up for identity, and if you are picked out, I shall charge you with murder.
Mathews: I've never had anything to do with murder or guns. When I read about it, I thought 'Lunatics.' I thought it was one of those vengeance things.
Drury: All I'm suggesting is you drove one of the motors.
Mathews: I wish I was fit enough to go on a job like this.

This was the big break for Drury, and what would prove to be the beginning of a nightmare for Murphy, Copper and McMahon. Drury, or his junior officers, had been hassling Alf Mathews' brother Albert, who was of course harbouring Alf in Ilford. Albert was told that if he could supply information as to where his brother was, he could have a share of the £5,000 reward money. Eventually this worked, and Albert called Drury and told him that Alf was in his house, therefore grassing on his brother. Police officers, including DC Laver, who had been circling Cooper, had gone to the front and back of Albert's house. They knocked and received no reply, but when Alf Mathews tried to escape out of the back door, they were ready for him, and took him to Drury at Luton police station, where the interview above was conducted. It is worth noting here that contrary to what he said, Mathews was far more than just the driver on the Luton Post Office job. In fact, Alf Mathews was the planner, the one who got the team together.

Evidence given to McMahon's lawyer Wendy Mantle later, in July 1971, shows just how deep was Mathews' involvement. Two men, Terry Leonard and Fred Stephens, swore on affidavit that Alf Mathews had approached them in 1968, the year before the Luton Post Office Murder, and invited them to take part in the job. Mathews had said that it would 'earn' them between £12,000 and £19,000 from the post office safe. It should be remembered that Mathews was the 'gelly' man, so would also have blown the safe. Mathews, Leonard and Stephens had gone to Luton and done a recce on the post office managed by Reginald Stevens.

According to Leonard and Stephens, Mathews had then told them that the intention was to threaten the postmaster (Stevens) with a gun, tie him up and use his keys. When they heard this, both Leonard and Stephens backed out, saying that they didn't want to take part if a gun was going to be used. Despite Mathews trying to change their minds, they had remained firm. Stephens also said that in 1969, the year of Stevens' murder, he had run into Mathews again by chance in prison: they were both on remand there independently for different offences. When Stephens asked him if the Luton job had been carried out, Mathews said that it hadn't, and that he was still looking for another firm to do it with him.

After the first interview on 22 October 1969, both Mathews' wife Florrie and brother Reg made statements to Drury's officers. Florrie confirmed that Mathews had been on the job, but that he wasn't the shooter. So Alf Mathews had obviously told his wife. The next evening, 23 October, Drury went back to Mathews and used Florrie's statement to unsettle him. Drury told Mathews that his answers to questions the previous day had been lies, and instructed him to read his wife's contrary statement. After this, Mathews was allowed to call his wife Florrie, and this was recorded by the police. The transcript shows that Mathews was panicking. Florrie was crying on the other end, and it ended with Mathews begging his brother Reg to bring Florrie down to Luton police station. Now Drury went in for the kill and had Mathews in for a second interview, during which they had a cup of tea. Mathews asked why his wife had given the statement:

> Drury: Because she wanted the truth to come out. She asked me to treat you fairly, and that's what I'm doing.
> Mathews: I know that if a man goes with some others, and they murder someone, they're all murderers.

Drury's next question is very ambiguous:

> Drury: That would depend on the circumstances. What did you have in mind?
> Mathews: I wouldn't entertain violence. [This goes against the later evidence of Leonard and Stephens, who said that Mathews was planning for a gun to be taken on the Luton job.]

Drury was reassuring in his reply, and after more protestations from Mathews, he laid out his position.

> Drury: Nobody is suggesting you used any violence. I'm quite prepared to believe that this was a blagging that went wrong, and you had no part in the actual shooting, but I don't know. The only people that know the full story are those that took part, and from my inquiries I think you are one of those people. What part you took, I don't know. The story you told yesterday was entirely false, as your wife says.

Mathews then asked if his brother Reg had made a statement. Reg would have had a different story about how he received the money for the Vauxhall, so would have contradicted Alf:

> Drury: We have taken one, and we will be taking another. You have spoken on the phone to him, and you know that he's not going to alibi you now. You know you're wife isn't going to alibi you either. Do you want to tell me the truth?

All of the exchanges above were not recorded on tape, but taken down in note form by another police officer sitting in. Taping technology did not exist in a practical way in 1969, but a reel-to-reel recording could have been made in that period. Incredibly, it would not be until 1984, and the passing of the Police and Criminal Evidence Act (PACE) that all police interviews had to be recorded. Policemen of Drury's era and before were therefore much less accountable. A bent policeman such as Drury was able to do many things off the record, and often not in a police station. For instance, the tailor who would confirm that Cooper had visited him about his suit on the day of the Luton Post Office Murder, part of Cooper's alibi, later said that Drury had interviewed him in his car. Drury had tried to convince the tailor that he had the date of Cooper's visit wrong, but the tailor stood firm. Such tactics were not used by Drury alone however, as we will see.

As Ludovic Kennedy pointed out in his book on the Luton Post Office Murder, *Wicked Beyond Belief*, that interview between Drury and Mathews on the evening of 23 October 1969 began at 8.02 p.m., and after some exchanges had been made, most included above, there was a note stating 'Pause: 8 minutes.' No further notes were taken after that, but the interview was entered as ending at 11.15 p.m. So what were Drury and Mathews talking about for the rest of that time and over the next two days while Mathews remained at Luton? As Ludovic Kennedy wrote in 1979, that time 'is the key to the Luton murder case'.

On 25 October, between 1.25 and 3.15 a.m., Mathews made a final statement to Drury, which was mostly untrue. Most importantly, Drury knew at the time that they were lies, and he worked with Mathews to concoct his story. In the statement, Mathews implicated Cooper, calling him by his real name, John, and mentioning where Cooper lived in Forest Gate, east London. The other two men in the gang were not named or described. The whole tone and words of Mathews' statement indicated that he had been tricked, and that the others, especially 'John', had led him astray. We now know that was far from the truth, that Mathews had assembled the firm who carried out the Luton Post Office Murder. Also that Cooper, McMahon and Murphy had nothing whatsoever to do with it.

In his statement, Mathews even said that while the search was on for him, he had gone to work as a builder every day, 'from morning till late at night'. Mathews said that this was because he was afraid that 'John' and the other men in the gang would come and 'do the same to me as they had done to the postmaster'. We know that Mathews had never gone to work in that time and that he was hiding in his brother Albert's house in Ilford. And Drury knew that too, on 25 October 1969, but let Mathews write it in his official statement. It is also possible that Drury dictated what had happened to Mathews.

Drury never did put Alf Mathews on an identity parade, despite knowing that he definitely took part in the attempted robbery that led to the murder of Reginald Stevens, and charging him with this. Added to this, Drury took a further statement from a Luton witness later that very same day, 25 October. This time, the sighting of Mathews as the getaway driver was omitted. Drury also took further statements from other Luton witnesses over the coming days and weeks, which also mysteriously changed in detail from the statements taken immediately after the murder on 10 September. Then Drury got Alf Mathews to go through photographs of known London criminals. Conveniently, Mathews chose the photos of Cooper (whom Mathews knew of course), McMahon and Murphy. Drury had what he needed, and the fit-up was on.

★ ★ ★

The day before Mathews was arrested, on 21 October 1969, Cooper had been visited at home by DC Laver. Laver was the same detective who had been fishing around Cooper before, as well as being at the arrest of Mathews. Cooper was told that Drury wanted to see him at Ponders End police station regarding the Luton Post Office Murder. They drove there in Cooper's red Mercedes, which had a 'soft top'. On the way, DC Laver asked if the car had ever had a 'hard top'. Cooper said it hadn't. It might be remembered that Herbert Andrews, one of the Luton witnesses, had said that the red sports car had a 'hard top'. So Laver was obviously trying to connect Cooper's car to the murder.

At the police station, Cooper was kept waiting for Drury to arrive. Cooper later remembered, 'It seemed that everybody was in awe of him before he made his entrance.' Drury obviously had some presence, as well as being a high-ranking officer, and this no doubt added to his aura and the sense of audacity he employed in his fit-ups and corruption. When Drury walked in, he made a big impression on Cooper, who later wrote that Drury's 'lips were thin and he gave the impression of a hard mouth. He had puffy eyes and a prominent jowl, and he looked tired.' Drury said that he had been told in a phone call (undoubtedly from an informant, if the call had ever happened), saying that Cooper was on the Luton team when Stevens had been killed. Cooper denied this of course, and did this at some length, writing down his movements on the day of the murder and signing it. Cooper was not charged:

> Cooper: I said that although I was a thief, shotgun robberies were hardly the sort of thing I went in for. He must have known this was true ...

Cooper also remembered that Drury said that he didn't think that Cooper was involved in the Luton murder. Drury had a good look at Cooper's red Mercedes, and then asked if Cooper would take part in an ID parade. The fact that Cooper was brought in for questioning the day before Alf Mathews was given his dodgy deal shows that Drury already had Cooper, and as we know McMahon and Murphy, in the frame for the Luton Post Office Murder. The coercion of Mathews and the fitting of facts in Mathews' statement shows that Drury's idea to implicate Cooper, McMahon and Murphy was planned in advance. It may well have been Cooper's red Mercedes which flagged him up in Drury's crafty mind, and the fact that Cooper was known to Mathews. As all three of them were already being looked into about other recent post office robberies, they were easy targets anyway.

Five days later, on 26 October, McMahon read in a newspaper that Mathews had been arrested and was relieved. But later that day, four detectives came to where he lived and took away some of his clothes. They asked him where he would be if Drury wanted to speak to him about the Luton job. This was of course ominous, and McMahon had never met Mathews.

Murphy was arrested and taken to Luton police station to see Drury on 29 October. They came for McMahon on 31 October. The police officers said that 'the Guv'nor' wanted to speak to him, and that Alf Mathews and Patrick 'Patsy' Murphy had already made statements and that they knew everything. Mathews had of course worked with Drury to implicate McMahon, Cooper and Murphy. But Murphy had certainly not made a statement implicating McMahon in any shape or form. McMahon's interview with Drury at Ponders End police station was short. McMahon recalled that Drury had a nose 'that one would normally associate with the first floor of the Thomas a Becket pub in the Old Kent Road'. At the time, there was a famous boxing gym there where the 1960s British Heavyweight Champion Henry Cooper used to train.

McMahon was put on an ID parade, and he was picked out by Mrs Crawley, a Luton witness. It might be remembered that Mrs Crawley had seen a lean, dark-haired man, 'perhaps in his late teens', running and jumping in the back of the green van, just after she heard the shots that killed Reginald Stevens. She had said, also in her statement to Luton police on 10 September 1969, within hours of the murder, that she 'wouldn't recognise him again'. Mrs Crawley had been talking with her friend Mrs Calvert in a garden some 65 yards from where Stevens was shot in the car park. Now, miraculously, facing a line of men, she was able to choose Michael McMahon, almost seven weeks later.

It would later come out that just over two weeks before the ID parade, on 14 October, Mrs Crawley had not been able to pick McMahon out of a group of suspect photographs. Also that not long before that 31 October ID parade, Drury had shown Mrs Crawley a photograph of McMahon, therefore blatantly leading a witness. McMahon was charged with murder. Murphy had also been identified as one of two men that she could have seen by Mrs Calvert, Mrs Crawley's friend.

On 4 November, Cooper was arrested and put on an ID parade at Luton police station before Alf Mathews and his wife Florrie. They both picked him out. Mathews said that Cooper was the man who had driven his red sports car to Luton on 10 September. Mathews' wife said that Cooper had been in their flat on both 9 and 10 September.

Both facts were lies, as although Cooper knew Mathews, had done a few jobs with him and had visited the Mathews' flat in Roman Road, that had been earlier in the year. As part of the deal, Drury had made sure that all the loose ends were tied up, with the full co-operation of Mathews and his wife. Florrie may have been coerced by Mathews, as Mathews faced a life sentence for murder if he did not take the deal. Cooper was charged with murder.

On 6 November 1969, Murphy was pulled out of an ID parade by Mathews, neither man ever having seen each other in their lives before. Murphy was charged. McMahon was also picked out by Mathews in a parade on 10 November, and after that he was also charged. All three men were now up for the murder of Reginald Stevens, with Mathews also charged with this. But as he was going to turn Queen's Evidence against Cooper, McMahon and Murphy in Drury's frame-up, he was likely to receive a far lighter sentence or none at all.

★ ★ ★

Drury would be busy in the next weeks, leaning on witnesses. First his men and then he, in his car, leant on Cooper's tailor, Morris Lerman, who was part of his alibi, but all were unsuccessful. Lerman later said of Drury's officers: 'They tried to turn me against him [Cooper]. They asked me how I would like it if one of my relatives had been shot in the guts.' Not a total waste of time, however, as under court law, the defence could not take a statement from the tailor if the prosecution got their first, which it had. Therefore, Drury had skilfully and malevolently insured that the tailor could not testify on Cooper's behalf at the trial. Drury also went to see Terry Langston, who had allegedly been looking after the shotgun for Michael Good, the one used to shoot Stevens. Drury stressed that a share of the £5,000 reward would be on offer, and that a married man (Stevens) had been murdered. But Langston repeated that he had never seen the gun.

Drury also went to the trouble of tightening his case against McMahon. McMahon was held on remand at Leicester Prison, and while he was there spent some time talking to two other inmates, Derek

Jackson and Thomas Weyers. On 20 November 1969, Jackson was given seven years and moved next to McMahon's cell. Weyers was in the cell on the other side of McMahon, and in a statement they said that they would communicate through a pipe which ran between all three cells. The police got to Jackson and Weyers, the latter of whom was already being contacted to speak in McMahon's defence by his lawyers. Soon both made a statement, saying that McMahon had confessed his part in the Luton Post Office Murder to them, not once, but several times. Jackson had even taken notes of what McMahon said.

At the trial, this evidence would be used against McMahon. Weyers would later have his thirty-three-month sentence for burglary reduced to a nine-month suspended sentence, which meant he was released. Weyers also received some of the reward. But in 1979, Ludovic Kennedy interviewed Thomas Weyers, who said that 'The details which I put into McMahon's mouth were all fed to me by Det. Sgt Horn. I said what I did because of the threats and promises made to me by Mr Horn and the local CID inspector.'

Back on 3 December 1969, Mathews had completed a much more detailed statement for Drury, this time naming and implicating Cooper, McMahon and Murphy. It was all lies of course. The trio of men who made up the real Luton gang in addition to Mathews, one of whom had fired the fatal shots that killed Reginald Stevens, were still at large and would remain so. Mathews' willingness to take the deal was obviously made easier by the threat of a life sentence. Mathews was not a criminal with the mental capacity to do a long sentence. Despite this, Mathews had put the Luton firm together. There is also evidence that he picked up the shotgun used in the murder, although Mathews was definitely not the shooter.

Added to this, there was Mathews' fear of the other three men, the real Luton team, and especially reprisals from their associates if he grassed them up. Finally, there was the inducement of a share of the £5,000 Post Office reward, as we will see. A villain who truly lived by the criminal code of not informing on accomplices would have reluctantly taken the fall, naming nobody and doing the life sentence. Mathews was a lifelong criminal, but not of such substance, and had previously lied to escape a longer stretch inside. On 19 March 1970, more than six months after the Luton Post Office Murder, David Cooper (John Disher), Michael McMahon and Patrick Murphy were found guilty of the murder of Reginald Stevens. They all received life sentences and a recommendation that they serve twenty years. They were all innocent of the charge, and the next years in prison would be traumatic ones, especially for Cooper and McMahon. If any more proof were needed of their innocence, all three were offered lesser sentences before the trial, as it was thought that murder convictions might not stick. This was because the theory was that the gun had probably gone off by accident. Cooper and McMahon had been offered the charge of conspiracy to rob, which would have got them five years at most, and Murphy, for whom the fitted-up evidence was more damning, a charge of manslaughter. All three of them had declined to take the deal.

Next, as the leading officer in the case, Drury had to inform the Post Office how it should pay out the reward money. This was how the £5,000 was split. The Luton witnesses Mrs Crawley and Mrs Calvert got £200 each, as did another Luton witness who had identified Murphy. Herbert Andrews, the commuter in Luton Train Station car park, got £400. Derek Jackson and Thomas Weyers, who had given false evidence against McMahon under police manipulation, received £500 apiece, as did Michael Good, the original owner of the murder weapon. Good was later considered by someone very well versed in the intricacies of the case of being highly likely to have taken part in the crime. Alf Mathews' brother Albert, who had harboured Alf before turning him in, got £500 too. Finally, Alf Mathews, the main plank of Drury's cover-up, the organiser of the Luton Post Office job and the driver on the day, got £2,000.

Even worse, Alf Mathews gave an interview with the investigative journalist William Thomson in 1971. Mathews, who was trying to get Thomson to secure him a newspaper deal for his 'life story', admitted after repeated questioning that Drury had taken half of his share, so £1,000. Drury had told Mathews that he had received shares from other reward recipients too. The fact is that Drury had specifically asked the Post Office to send the cheques for Alf Mathews, Albert Elliott and

Michael Good to him personally, for him to pass on. This is confirmed in a letter sourced by Ludovic Kennedy from the Post Office to Drury on 20 May 1970. Sickeningly, the letter ends with the Post Office official writing: 'I should not wish to let this opportunity pass without offering you my personal thanks and congratulations on the successful outcome of the murder inquiry.' Congratulations were indeed due to Det. Chief Supt Drury, for a masterclass in police corruption, which meant that three entirely innocent men were starting their life sentences.

Incidentally, Jimmy Humphreys, Drury's later friend then enemy, whom we have met already several times, made a statement to a Det. Sgt Stagg in Gartree Prison in Liverpool in 1975 where he was then serving eight years. Humphreys said that Drury had told him that he had had 'a good drink' from the informants' money in the Luton Post Office Murder. We will be meeting Jimmy Humphreys again shortly.

★ ★ ★

The 1970s saw a series of legal appeals for Cooper, McMahon and Murphy. On 26 February 1971, the first appeal was dismissed, and they had to wait until 13 November 1973 for the second. For Cooper and McMahon, this was too dismissed, but for Murphy justice was finally done. His conviction was quashed on new witness evidence and therefore Mathews' evidence, which had done so much to convict all three men at the original trial, was called into question regarding Murphy. Incredibly, the Appeal Judges did not feel that it also called Mathews' evidence into serious question regarding Cooper and McMahon. But for Patrick Murphy, it was release from prison after more than three and a half years, and also from a waking nightmare.

The second and third appeals by Cooper and McMahon were frustratingly and infuriatingly dismissed on 12 February 1975 and 22 July 1976 respectively. By the time of the latter appeal, Drury was already facing preliminary trials for other corruption, the story of which will be told in the next four chapters. Due to this, Cooper and McMahon and their legal teams were told not to raise questions about Drury's then alleged corruption in their case at the appeal, as it could prejudice

Drury's other pending trial. This was the period when one of Cooper's brothers heckled Drury at Bow Street Magistrates' Court, as seen in the Prologue. After Drury had been convicted on unrelated corruption charges in 1977, the fifth appeal of Cooper and McMahon, including evidence against Drury, was rejected. It seemed that all hope was lost.

Prison had taken its toll on both Cooper and McMahon. Being innocent yet convicted of murder is one of the worst possible scenarios – especially when they knew that the police had framed them with the aid of a guilty criminal. To exacerbate this sense of deep and wilful unfairness, the legal establishment was not seeing the truth, or perhaps was unwilling to see it. Both men suffered terribly, were changed immeasurably, their hopes dashed in appeal after appeal. But their families, friends and legal teams remained loyal and offered the support they needed. While in prison, both Cooper and McMahon independently wrote long manuscripts telling their story and plight. The words of both of them, at the end of their respective manuscripts, are very poignant:

> David Cooper: I shall be vindicated. I am more certain of that than I am of anything in my life. And although it is a slow, and at times agonising, road I tread, the time will come when I shall be heard and cleared of the indictment held against me.

> Michael McMahon: I will not conveniently go away. In or out of prison I will relentlessly fight my case until my conviction for the murder of Reginald Stevens is finally quashed.

In his manuscript, Cooper also wrote: 'I have learned not to think too deeply about Mathews, his wife, Drury, etc. at night, because the questions which these people raise are not conducive to a good night's sleep.' It was these manuscripts which were given to the legendary writer, broadcaster and miscarriage of justice campaigner Sir Ludovic Kennedy. Kennedy had already most famously secured a posthumous pardon for Timothy Evans, five years after the publication of his classic work of crime reportage *Ten Rillington Place*. This was about the murders perpetrated in that Notting Hill house by the depraved serial killer John Christie, one murder for which, that of his own baby Geraldine, Evans was unjustly hanged. Evans' case also had many dubious police procedural elements. Kennedy saw that Cooper and McMahon's stories were true and shocking, and he agreed to take on the case in 1979.

His resulting book, *Wicked Beyond Belief,* was published in June 1980, and miraculously Cooper and McMahon were released just over three weeks later on 18 July 1980, although their convictions were not quashed. Kennedy had used his legal and governmental connections to get the book read by influential people in the Home Office, and the Home Secretary Willie Whitelaw ordered the releases. Enormous credit should be given to the late Sir Ludovic Kennedy for the forensic and compelling way in which he laid out this miscarriage of justice in his book, and got Cooper and McMahon released after five appeals had been rejected.

Willie Whitelaw later told Kennedy, a personal friend, that he had wanted to quash the convictions too, but the then Lord Chief Justice, Geoffrey Lane, had objected. What is even more worrying is why the duplicity of Drury, who was already serving a prison sentence for unrelated corruption, and Alf Mathews, who should have now served a lengthy sentence, having colluded with Drury to convict Murphy, Cooper and McMahon, were not fully investigated. Mathews served no time for the Luton Post Office Murder, despite being the planner and the driver, and probably the intended 'gelly' man. We know that Mathews knew that a gun was going to be used in the year previous to the crime, so he would have received at least a manslaughter sentence under joint enterprise.

Drury too was never punished legally for his malicious corruption in this case. He should have served another lengthy sentence for it. So, why was there no independent inquiry of Drury's 1969–70 investigation into the murder of Reginald Stevens? Considering that the then Home Secretary was moved to release Cooper and McMahon in 1980, it has to be said that there seems to have been a closing of ranks at the highest levels, a brushing of this heinous injustice under the quilted carpet of the Establishment.

But in fact Drury's corruption in the Luton Post Office Murder would come back to haunt him indirectly. It might be remembered that Patrick 'Patsy' Murphy's father Steven was a close friend of the gangster Joey Pyle. It was Pyle who would tip off the *Sunday People* newspaper in 1972, giving a revelation about Drury's association with Soho gangland which would trigger the beginning of Drury's long fall from grace. It has usually been reported that Pyle had done this as he was upset with the police after he felt that he had been fitted up on a gun charge in relation to a man named Fred Sewell. Sewell was a London car dealer who had shot dead Det. Supt Gerald Richardson in Blackpool in August 1971, after an armed raid on a jeweller's there. But in his memoirs years later, Pyle wrote that it was because Patrick Murphy had got life and he knew that he was innocent. For this reason, Drury had to be brought down:

> Pyle: Years later the story would go round that I was so pissed off about being fitted up with the guns over the Sewell stuff that I spilled the beans on Drury out of revenge, but it was never like that. It was just to help a friend get off a murder charge.

Although they had been released after serving nearly eleven years, the whole trauma had taken a toll on both David Cooper and Michael McMahon. In January 1993, Cooper was found dazed and wandering aimlessly with a large cut at the back of his head. It was never determined whether he had fallen or been hit. In September of that year, Cooper died, aged just 51. Michael McMahon would also die prematurely, aged 55, on 25 June 1999. It was his birthday.

Both men had been almost broken by Drury's fit-up, suffering much mental anguish and turmoil. In May 2000, Cooper's long-time lawyer Gareth Peirce put the cases of Cooper and McMahon forward for another appeal. Pierce wrote: 'The writer of these submissions has no doubt that the life and health of each was drastically affected by the eleven years each spent in torment in prison.' That appeal, the sixth, finally opened on 31 July 2003 and on the next day, the convictions of Cooper and McMahon were quashed, more than thirty-three years after they had been given, and almost thirteen years after their release. The late Sir Ludovic Kennedy was in court that day, and said that he was delighted, but that it should have happened years before. It was finally justice, but both Cooper and McMahon were already dead, and their families had had to deal with all that despair too, for so many years.

★ ★ ★

There is a final interesting insight into the Luton Post Office Murder, which has never been known before. Inside the Metropolitan Police Files accessed by this author under the Freedom of Information Act, there is a statement made by Drury, on 10 March 1972, almost two years after Murphy, Cooper and McMahon started their life sentences. Drury was giving an internal police statement in relation to other corruption allegations made against him, for which and more he would eventually be convicted.

Therefore, the Luton Post Office Murder was not relevant to this interview. Inextricably, Drury brings it up, with no provocation or any question about it being asked. Drury mentions *The Sunday Times* newspaper and another regional newspaper, the *Redbridge Gazette*, and two particular unnamed journalists, who had been 'digging', as part of a campaign to get Patrick Murphy released. This had of course happened in the November of the following year, four months earlier. Jimmy Humphreys is mentioned, as he was central to the corruption charges then facing Drury, and one reporter was obviously sniffing around Humphreys too.

It's easy to picture the scene. Drury is under pressure for his career and perhaps even his freedom, and he sees that the whole corrupt web he has woven could be unpicked. He gets his say in about the Luton Post Office Murder, in a formal statement, in case it comes up in police inquiries into his professional misconduct. Accusations he makes about a journalist having a grudge against him, and who he claims is out to get him, is a nice touch. Drury's devious mind must have been grafting overtime. This part of Drury's statement is worth quoting in full here:

The other matter which I wish to bring to attention is this, and it relates to the murder of Reginald Stevens, the postmaster who was shot dead at Luton on 10th September, 1969, a matter which I was responsible for investigating whilst attached to the Murder Squad. Three men were convicted of this crime and since conviction, one of them, namely Patrick Colin Murphy, has, through his father, Stephen George Murphy, been endeavouring to obtain a fresh trial, on the grounds that he was wrongly convicted. In support for the movement for a new trial, two reporters, one from the 'Redbridge Gazette' and one from 'The Sunday Times', who at this stage I do not wish to name, conducted a newspaper campaign on behalf of Murphy. In October of last year, I think the 16th, they called on me at New Scotland Yard, to discuss what they considered to be fresh evidence in the case of Murphy. I told them that if they were in possession of fresh evidence, they should hand it to the solicitors responsible for Murphy's defence or, if they preferred, I would report the matter to the Director of Public Prosecutions. After a general conversation they left me and I have seen neither of them since. I have now received reliable information that the reporter from the 'Redbridge Gazette' who, I have ascertained, is no longer employed by them but now employed by the 'Sunday People' has approached a man currently on bail in South London, who has a relative working on the 'People' asking him if he knows Humphreys, which he does, as he, the reporter, wished to 'fit me up' because I am supposedly alleged to have been responsible for him being sacked from the 'Redbridge Gazette'. The man on bail refused to have any part of this. I am still making enquiries in an endeavour to gain absolute confirmation of what has taken place and if and when I do I will report the matter officially ...

Drury's ploy was to plant the seed of doubt about the motivations of the journalist investigating the safety of Murphy's conviction, to imply that this journalist had a personal vendetta against him. Of course, Drury knew full well that Murphy's conviction, and also Cooper and McMahon's convictions, were unsafe, as he had fitted all three up. By getting it on the Metropolitan Police record by means of his internal investigation statement, Drury was laying calculated foundations.

This was in case the unnamed journalist who had smelt a fat stinking rat in the corrupt framework of Drury's Luton Post Office Murder convictions came up with real allegations of corruption against him which could stick.

That journalist now worked for the *Sunday People*, and that newspaper had started the exposure of Drury's connections to Soho vice shortly before, after Joey Pyle's tip-off. For Drury, it was obviously all about getting it on the record, and in this he succeeded. Just six days after Drury's statement, the reference made about the journalist found its way into the 16 March 1972 report made by the Metropolitan Police No.1 Area Inspectorate, just one of ninety-six points, for the eyes of the Deputy Commissioner:

> A news reporter, formerly employed by the 'Redbridge Gazette', who now works for the 'Sunday People', might be vindictive towards him [Drury] because he was allegedly responsible for the reporter being dismissed from his earlier employment.

This author believes that the 'man currently on bail in South London' mentioned by Drury in his statement was the late Joey Pyle. The journalist in question has been identified, but could not be traced now for comment, so it would be unfair to publish his name here.

So what did Drury do in the investigation of the Luton Post Office Murder? He venally and wilfully framed three men, one of whom served almost four years in prison, with the other two serving almost eleven years, ruining their lives, hopes and dreams. In the words of the late Sir Ludovic Kennedy, 'In the Luton case, there was no question of the officer in charge, Det. Chief Supt (later Commander) Kenneth Drury believing that Cooper and McMahon were guilty ... he knew for a fact that they were innocent.' Drury's handiwork also led to the bribing of two prison inmates to give false evidence against McMahon. Drury also convinced a witness to alter his evidence against Cooper and got his men to work on another whilst at the same time preventing him from being a witness for the defence. Drury made the picking out of McMahon in an ID parade much more likely by identifying him to the witness prior to the parade, and held back the evidence of two witnesses whose evidence was supportive of Cooper and McMahon from their defence team. Finally, Drury did an unbelievably corrupt deal with a guilty man who had planned and taken part in the failed armed robbery in Luton that day which led to the death of Reginald Stevens, taking a large share of the reward money for himself.

Apart from profiting financially, Drury had got three convictions and seemingly turned another guilty man. It was a very high-profile case that had been rightly greeted with widespread public revulsion and had put the Metropolitan Police under enormous pressure to catch the culprits. Drury now looked like a 'murder whizz', and his flabby frame had moved further up the greasy pole of promotion. They were excellent 'nicks' in the eyes of his superiors, but the question has to be asked about how culpable of corruption Drury's subordinate police officers were in the Luton Post Office Murder frame-up too. But then, they would say that they were just following orders, the orders of Det. Chief Supt Drury.

Just over a year after the unsafe convictions of Murphy, Cooper, and McMahon, Kenneth Drury was a commander and head of the Flying Squad.

3

THE SOHO CONNECTION

Soho, West London, Early 1970s

THE INNER-CITY VILLAGE of vice streets of Soho are buzzing, and shady-looking men stand in doorways, demanding a £1 entrance fee for a show, a strip, the allure of female flesh. Membership books are signed with fictitious names, including film stars, cartoon characters and dictators. Topless bars, sensational revues, international artistes, it's all here if you want a peep, a peek or a gander – jiggling, shimmying and pouting. Forbidden fruit, some more bruised than others, some bored, some on autopilot, some inspired, depending on the venue. For fifty pence you can't expect a beauty. Yes mister, you've got to speculate to ejaculate.

Down murky tunnel-like corridors, through the plastic curtain, there she is, on the chair, the men sat round her, some of them with empty expressions and wide-lapelled suits as if watching the television news, others scruffy and excited and leaning forward for inspection of nipples. But all fight for a front row seat when somebody leaves, satiated. Will she go all the way? It's choky, smoke-filled, mixed with the abrasive smell of Just Musk and Aquamanda scents. Stylish men nervously check the time on a Pulsar, the first digital watch, in the dimly lit bargain basements. But if you've got money to burn up west you can do it in comfortable lounge nitespots too. You'll be served by topless ladies saving for the future or supplementing income, though for that you're talking £1.75 plus drinks, in some places fake champagne at 30 bob a glass. Then watch gaudily dressed ladies in show-all solos, but some show their class by not opening their legs when the record or band playing for their act comes to an end.

Not far from here, there's the Hogarth Club, one of the places where Commander Kenneth Drury of the Flying Squad meets Soho face Jimmy Humphreys. The Premier too, where other police–villain transactions take place, and the White Horse pub, where Humphreys and one of the most powerful men in Soho, Bernie Silver, leave bent police officers their payments. But this isn't the time for business. Striptease cabaret is all the rage, eighteen beautiful girls on offer over there, and if you've got the notes, in some places you can take away. But to those who know Soho there's also an undercurrent of menace in the air.

★ ★ ★

The names of the clubs give the full flavour of Soho in this period – the Blue City Revue Club, the Big Toe, the Blue Moon, the Carnival, the Carousel, the Casbah, Casino de Paris, the Compton Cinema Club, the Dolls House, the Galaxy, the Geisha, the Gargoyle, the Gigi, the Queen's, Maxim's, the Morocco, the Nell Gwynne, the Perfumed Garden, the Red Mill, Taboo, etc., etc. All over Old Compton Street, Frith Street, Dean Street, Berwick Street, Greek Street, Brewer Street, Great Windmill Street, Walker's Court, Wardour Street, Gerrard Street, Peter Street, Carlisle Street, and more.

Incidentally, in the early 1970s the Gargoyle and the Nell Gwynne on the corner of Dean and Meard Streets were run by Don Ward, who would set up the famous Comedy Store at the former in 1979, graduating from tits to titters. Ward still runs the London Comedy Store in a different location, and also has branches in Manchester and Mumbai, India. In a recent interview on BBC Radio, Ward said that the entertainer Larry Grayson and singer Ruby Murray performed at the Gargoyle. In 1973 at the Gargoyle, Ward apparently met Penny Sutton, then recent author of *The Stewardesses* and *The Stewardesses Down Under.* Sutton published an article, *The Sutton Report*, about her trip around the striptease clubs of Soho that day in *Penthouse* magazine. It seems that Penny Sutton was the pen name of Christopher Wood, who later wrote the screenplays for *Confessions of a Window Cleaner* and the James Bond films *The Spy Who Loved Me* and *Moonraker*. This author approached Don Ward for an interview about Soho in the 1970s, but Mr Ward declined.

There had been prostitution, striptease clubs, and pornographic bookshops in Soho for decades. In the 1920s, the Sabinis had their base at Admiral Duncan pub on Old Compton Street. This pub was nail-bombed in a homophobic attack in 1999 with fatalities; the author was working in a nearby bookshop and felt the ground shake. Later came the Messinas, Billy Hill and Jack Spot Comer. Comer had an infamous and vicious hand-to-hand-to-knife fight with a Soho gangster of Italian origin named Albert Dimes in August 1955. They fought all the way down Frith Street and then tumbled into a greengrocer's on Old Compton Street. It became known as the 'Fight That Never Was'. Later still came the Syndicate of the late 1950s, taking us up to the early 1970s, where we find ourselves now.

The Obscene Publications Squad had started life in 1932 as the 8 Area Clubs and Vice Unit, soon after the conviction of Sergeant Goddard for his Soho corruption. But the Dirty Squad of the 1960s and early 1970s had really been in that form since the late 1940s, early 1950s. Just as the Ghost Squad of the late 1940s had spawned the new autonomous Flying Squad, the Dirty Squad became more independent then too. So the immediate post-war years had sown the roots of corruption, which took two decades to grow into the rotten juggernaut of the late 1960s and early 1970s.

It was the revolution which took place in Britain in the mid-late 1960s, in music, literature, film, fashion, social and sexual mores and in culture generally that led to Soho truly becoming a massively lucrative vice mecca, through prostitution, stripping and pornography. Back then it was called the 'permissive society' by the Establishment. Formerly repressed sexuality, and suppressed mediums to express it, opened up as never before, although the contraceptive pill had been available to buy since 1961. As we saw earlier, the Metropolitan Police in the form of the Obscene Publications Squad, aka the Dirty Squad, was busier raiding art gallery bookshops for naughty picture books in the late 1960s than taking down the illegal hard-core pornography. Often imported, it was sold on the streets of Soho. As we will see, there were very unsavoury reasons why the Dirty Squad often turned a blind eye, especially as it was supposed to be enforcing the stringent Obscene Publications Act of 1959.

The most famous use of the 1959 Act was the furore caused by the trial over publication of D.H. Lawrence's literary erotic novel *Lady Chatterley's Lover* in 1960. The prosecuting counsel said in court: 'Is it a book that you would wish your wife or servants to read?' The verdict resulted in the publisher Penguin being able to legally publish it, and it subsequently sold 2 million copies in 1961 alone. Of course, the kind of graphic pornography which the Dirty Squad allowed to be sold in the late 1960s and early 1970s was in a far more extreme league than Lady Chatterley cavorting with her gamekeeper Mellors.

The law which the Dirty Squad was supposed to enforce at this time was the Obscene Publications Act 1964, which amended the original legislation of five years earlier. The 1959 Act stipulated that it was punishable on summary conviction or an indictment for 'any person who, whether for gain or not, publishes an obscene article'. The 1964 Act added 'or who has an obscene article for publication for gain (whether gain to himself or another).' The later Act also went into details about how the obscene material would be 'forfeited' or seized.

In his 1978 memoirs, the recently retired Met Police Commissioner Sir Robert Mark gave his view about the policing of pornography:

> The law on pornography is a mess … My own inclination is that if there is to be a change in law, that the emphasis should be on control of display rather than prohibition. I am not competent to say whether pornography depraves or corrupts … But I can say what is likely to offend and although I am not in favour of prohibition, I do not see why people should be needlessly offended by display. Control of display will not, however, be easy. Definition of that which is offensive will be difficult.

But this was an entirely separate issue to the corrupt machinations of the Dirty Squad, as Mark knew and felt very strongly.

We will see how the Dirty Squad allowed such obscene publications to be openly sold in Soho after and long before 1964. Also, how when pornography was seized from an 'unconnected' operator, it often went straight into the hands of a favoured operator, the latter being those paying corrupt Dirty Squad officers money. It was a clever and outrageous racket, and the autonomy of the Dirty Squad, just like the Flying Squad, allowed this to run for decades. Dirty Squad corruption began at least six years before the Obscene Publications Act 1959, and for eight years after the 1964 Act. It only ended with the huge Metropolitan Police corruption shakedown under Sir Robert Mark, which took the pornography brief away from the CID (the Dirty Squad) and gave it to the uniform branch.

Stripping clubs and pornographic bookshops proliferated in this era in Soho, and while for many a visit was still furtive and forbidden, it was also racy and adrenaline-inducing. A December 1974 report in the Metropolitan Police files, written in the past tense as there had just been that massive shakedown of both criminals and police, shows what was necessary for an operator of a porn bookshop to get into the business. 'As was the case with prostitution and other vice activities in Soho the key factor was the acquisition and control of suitable premises.' Operators such as Bernie Silver and 'Big Frank' Mifsud of the Syndicate, Jimmy Humphreys and others had to be shrewd property speculators. Both freehold and leasehold properties were bought, though usually the latter, to trade in dirty books and magazines. This required serious capital, and also involved very sizeable payments to the police. But the profits were enormous, so the outlay made by vice operators was justified as business expenses.

The business of pornography is explained in that same Met report. 'The pornographic business consisted of two groups of people (a) the persons who controlled the shops which were the retail outlet and (b) the wholesale suppliers.' Silver, Mifsud, Humphreys and John 'Eric' Mason were in the former category, running porn shops. Other operators were wholesale suppliers, such as Gerald Citron, Charles Julian (real name Charles A. Marandola from Las Vegas), Evan 'Big' Jeff Phillips and the, until now, publicly undocumented, due to the Met Police files being closed, Pieter Mulder. We will learn more about Mulder's Soho connections with Jimmy Humphreys later.

The way that pornographic bookshops, colloquially known as 'dirty bookshops', were run at the time was explained in a statement that leading porn retailer Jimmy Humphreys gave to the police in the early 1970s, and summarised in the same December 1974 report in the Metropolitan Police files. Humphreys:

> The shop usually consisted of a front room and a back room partitioned by a screen of some kind. Normally girlie magazines etc. would be kept in the front room and any hard porn in the rear. However, because of the reluctance of customers to go to the rear of the premises the shop turnover could be increased substantially if the hard porn books, films etc. were placed in the front of the shop.'

It was simple and logical reasoning, and obviously worked.

But Humphreys had also said in his statement that the Metropolitan Police were very influential regarding which porn retailers were favoured, in the form of the Dirty Squad. The report continues:

> Considerable feeling was aroused ... according to Humphreys, as to why some shops were apparently 'allowed' to have hard porn in the front room without any action being taken by the Obscene Publications Squad.

It had taken Humphreys a long time to develop his porn business. As we know, Humphreys had been in the striptease club game since his release from prison in 1962, and had prospered, with the help of the business acumen of his wife June 'Rusty' Humphreys. But pornography was another matter, as Humphreys soon realised. He had to have approval – a licence from the the Dirty Squad – in order to operate effectively in the area. This involved not just illicit payment, but also an introduction by major criminals already licensed, to vouch for his suitability.

There was no bigger player in Soho vice at that time than Bernie Silver, co-head of the Syndicate with 'Big Frank' Mifsud. Silver would be Humphreys' entrance into big-time Soho pornography, which would make Humphreys what was called the 'Porn King'. Silver and Mifsud, aside from their extensive strip club interests, were also the major players in prostitution, having moved into the area once governed by the Messinas. This had been Silver's aim since he worked as a runner for the Messinas and moved into Soho from the Brick Lane area of the East End in the mid-late 1950s. Naturally, the help of Silver, referred to in the Metropolitan Police files as 'a notorious ponce', would cost Humphreys a great deal financially as well as in peace of mind.

There were also other vice operators in and around Soho at the time who would figure prominently in police corruption in the early-mid 1970s. Some of them had been making illicit regular payments to officers since the early 1950s, in increasing amounts as their criminal activities became more successful.

* * *

Until 1972, the Obscene Publications Squad was attached to COC1 (West End Central), and had a maximum of fifteen officers at any one time, including the sub-divisions at Vine Street and Bow Street police stations. The focus of these officers was to target illegal pornography, make arrests of retailers and suppliers, and shut down premises. Soho was the epicentre of pornography, and as the Met files show, between 1 January 1971 and 9 March 1972, a period of just over fourteen months, there were thirty proceedings made against indecent exhibitions at bookshops, an average of just over two a month. Nine of these proceedings were brought by West End Central, nineteen by Vine Street, and two by Bow Street. Considering the number of pornographic bookshops in Soho at the time, and the volume of hard-core pornographic material on sale, this is a poor strike rate. In the same period, there were just ten proceedings made against unlicensed public music and dancing at striptease clubs.

Silver and Mifsud's Gigi Club was raided twice in January 1971, their Keyhole Club once in January 1971 and again in June 1971. Both these clubs had suffered firebomb attacks in 1966–67, as we saw earlier. But the number of arrests made by the Dirty Squad was poor, and shows a need to 'keep up appearances', ticking over with the odd arrest, rather than a real clampdown as required by law. The law was of course what Metropolitan Police officers were expected to uphold. The Dirty Squad was riddled with corruption, and the Head of the Squad, Det. Supt Alfred 'Wicked Bill' Moody, would be convicted of corruption and receive a hefty prison sentence, as would his successor as Head, Det. Chief Inspector George Fenwick. Commander Wallace 'Wally' Virgo, a member of the Dirty Squad himself in the early 1960s, then Head of the Murder Squad (pre Drury), in overall command of COC1 from 1 April 1970, also had his nose in the trough. Virgo was no fool. He oversaw all the elite squads with real independence, nine in all, the Dirty Squad and Flying Squad among them. These were just the highest-ranking officers in and connected to the Dirty Squad, but there were others too.

Moody had joined West End Central in late 1965 as a detective inspector, and was soon making criminal contacts and organising his illegal and systematic licensing and protection system. A particularly close corrupt relationship was forged between Moody and the pornographer John 'Eric' Mason. This man should not be confused with the already mentioned Eric Mason, a member of the Kray firm, and a far heavier character. In December 1966, Moody was promoted to detective chief inspector, and in June 1968 he became a detective superintendent. He finally reached the rank of detective chief superintendent.

Moody would also be involved in the police response to the media's drawing of first police blood. This would also be the first of the newspaper crusades of the late 1960s and early 1970s which exposed the deep roots and widespread nature of Met Police corruption. It was *The Times*, Britain's oldest newspaper, which got the first scoop, on 29 November 1969. This was exactly the time when Det. Chief Supt Drury was completing his frame-up of Murphy, Cooper and McMahon for the Luton Post Office Murder. It published a shocking story about officers of C9, the Provincial Police Crime Branch. This exposé would become known as the *Times* Inquiry.

The journalists Garry Lloyd and Julian Mounter asserted in the article that they 'believed' that Det. Inspector Bernard Robson, Det. Sgt John Symonds and Det. Sgt Gordon Harris had taken bungs for dropping charges, making court evidence more lenient to criminals, and allowing a criminal to continue operating without curtailing his activities. The journalists had got the police officers bang to rights, taking photos and tape-recording a meeting with a petty criminal, Michael Perry. The author James Morton points out that Perry was advised to go to the *Times* by none other than Joey Pyle.

It was Det. Sgt Symonds whose comments on the recordings were truly damning. To the criminal Michael Perry he said:

> Always let me know straightaway if you need anything because I know people everywhere – because I'm in a little firm in a firm. Don't matter where, anywhere in London I can get on the phone to someone I know I can trust, that talks the same as me. And if he's not the right person that can do it, he'll know the person that can.

Symonds also stated elsewhere in the conversation, 'We've got more villains in our game than you've got in yours, you know.' The phrase 'firm within a firm' was the one that entered the public consciousness the most. The bribes taken by the three officers were later proved to only total £275, of which £150 related to Symonds. But the fact that the insipidly corrupt Moody was seconded from the Dirty Squad for a while to internally look into the allegations is laughable in hindsight. The levels of corruption that Moody himself was later convicted of made the crimes of Symonds, Robson and Harris insignificant. But the greatest damage of the *Times* piece to the Metropolitan Police was that readers could see that serving police officers, in the CID, spoke like the criminals they were supposed to be catching, did murky deals with them, and indeed seemed proud of doing so.

In fact, there was other cause for concern regarding alleged obstruction within the Metropolitan Police. The then Home Secretary and future Prime Minister Jim Callaghan called in Frank Williamson, the Inspector of Constabulary for Crime, to oversee the *Times* Inquiry overall. An Inspector of Constabulary was not a police officer and had no police powers, and could not directly give orders to any officer, but had to approach senior officers with any findings. Williamson, a long-time friend of the future Commissioner Robert Mark, would retire not long after, thoroughly disillusioned. Williamson later said that he had encountered serious obstruction from inside the CID in his efforts to get to the heart of the matter, and that in his opinion Moody had been attached to the *Times* Inquiry in order to scupper it.

Williamson said he was ostracised by the top ranks, and this was confirmed by another friend, Leonard 'Nipper' Read, who had brought down the Krays in the previous year. Read said in his memoirs that while Williamson was going through his troubles on the *Times* Inquiry, they had to meet in a pub instead of at New Scotland Yard in order to talk frankly. Read also recalled that Williamson had said that he was concerned about the calibre of the police officers investigating the affair, especially Det. Chief Supt Moody. Added to this, another Det. Chief Supt, Fred Lambert, had been removed from the *Times* Inquiry early on. Lambert was removed by none other than Commander Wally Virgo, who would be convicted for corruption along with Moody later.

The fact that Symonds boasted of his wide bent reach in London was a hint of the institutionalised corruption which would be unearthed in the next few years. The legal proceedings against the officers were drawn out, and it wasn't until 3 March 1972 that Robson was given seven years, and Harris six years in prison. By this time, Kenneth Drury, Head of the Flying Squad, was also being investigated for corruption after a newspaper article exposed him, and shortly the Drugs Squad would be plagued by allegations too, after an article in the *Sunday Times*. Incidentally, in 1969 the Lancashire Constabulary Drugs Squad had also come under the spotlight, and six officers went to trial. According to Sir Robert Mark in his memoirs, Flying Squad officers were arrested in Lancashire at this time.

Ex-Det. Sgt Symonds of C9, the other officer in the *Times* Inquiry, had gone on the run, and came back to give himself up eight years later. He went to Africa and became a soldier, and then when he fell ill, on to Australia and New Zealand. At his 1981 trial, for some reason Symonds only received eighteen months, far less than the other two convicted officers, despite being on the run for eight years. Symonds alleged that he had been tipped off to go on the run during the *Times* Inquiry by none other than Det. Chief Supt 'Wicked Bill' Moody, who of course had been put in charge of the day-to-day operations of the inquiry for a spell. Symonds said in court that he had been told by Moody's junior officers, who were obviously relaying Moody's message, to 'leave the country'. By this time, Moody was already serving a long sentence for Soho corruption. But if it is true, Frank Williamson's claim that Moody had been attached to the *Times* Inquiry to 'sabotage' it is given stronger collaborative credence, and implicates Virgo.

The late 1960s through to the late 1970s is widely seen as the high point of British investigative journalism. Without that generation of brave and diligent journalists, the fact that the Metropolitan Police, especially the top squads, was riddled with corruption, might never have been known publicly, or even cleaned up internally. It was an example of how media pressure and public exposure can sometimes be the only route to the truth in a society that values freedom of speech. Any measures to limit that freedom could lead to cover-ups of corruption.

From 1969 until 23 October 1972, Moody was in charge of the Dirty Squad. Det. Chief Supt (later Commander) Kenneth Drury would soon be the head of the Flying Squad. The scene was all set for the most systemic corruption ever in the history of the Metropolitan Police. This would make the infamous activities of 'Tanky' Challenor in the early 1960s, the suspicions around the Flying Squad in the 1920s, 1930s, 1940s and 1950s, Det. George Goddard in Soho in the 1920s, and even the shocking malpractices exposed in the great police trials of 1877 seem amateurish in comparison. But the culture which really allowed the rot to set in had been developing since the late 1940s and the Ghost Squad. Like that template of a largely autonomous squad of seemingly elite officers, the Flying Squad and the Dirty Squad, at the centre of this pinnacle of impropriety, had real power and were not answerable as were other Metropolitan Police divisions. These elite squads had too much control and the bent coppers within them abused it audaciously.

But perhaps in retrospect there was another warning sign related to the *Times* Inquiry of late 1969 and early 1970. That is the fact that other officers, widely considered as honest, were either naïve, blinkered or simply turned a blind eye to the corruption they saw. This meant it could fester unchallenged. Frank Williamson had informed Assistant Commissioner (Crime) Peter Brodie, who had been at that very senior rank since 1966, that Det. Chief Supt Bill Moody was driving cars supplied by the Soho vice operator Jimmy Humphreys. Humphreys would soon be Commander Kenneth Drury of the Flying Squad's special friend too.

It would later be confirmed that a car that Moody drove had indeed come from Humphreys. Brodie, against whom there is no evidence of dishonesty, said that he wasn't interested in the matter. It should also be said that Williamson and Brodie had a strained relationship. Could Brodie have been frightened of dealing with the matter? Had the claws of corruption infiltrated so deep that senior officers were afraid to make a stand?

Sir Robert Mark, who in 1972 would become Met Police Commissioner and the scourge of corruption, wrote about Brodie in his memoirs. 'The trouble was that he believed too many of his subordinates to be untainted by corruption or other wrongdoing. He was incapable of seeing or believing the failings of many of those on whom he relied for advice.' A great pity, as perhaps if the bent cops could have been caught and rooted out internally, the massive damage to the reputation of the Metropolitan Police which would be exposed publicly could have been limited. As Edmund Burke said, 'The only thing necessary for the triumph of evil is for good men to do nothing.'

There is a final disturbing insight into the state of the Metropolitan Police and specifically the Flying Squad at that time. Frank Williamson later recounted that just before he retired in 1971, he made an inspection of the Essex Constabulary. It will be remembered that the three police officers from C9 involved in the *Times* Inquiry, Det. Inspector Robson, Det. Sgt Symonds and Det. Sgt Harris, were yet to face trial. Their defence counsels were doing everything they could to discredit the taped and photographic evidence against them.

On his inspection in Brentwood, Essex, Williamson was told by a Det. Inspector Larby, who had been in C9 in late 1969, that Det. Sgt Robson had admitted his guilt about the intimidation of the small-time villain Michael Perry, who had later gone to *The Times*. Det. Sgt Robson had said this in conversation at work on the day that the *Times* article was published. This related to the planting of gelignite for safe-breaking, which would presumably have given Robson leverage to demand more money. At early committal hearings in the case, other police officers had said in court that this incident had never happened. The implication was that there had been an orchestrated cover-up. Even worse, Larby told Williamson that he had already told his Chief Constable, John Nightingale. Nothing had been done. Larby's statement was taken by a detective chief superintendent of the Essex force.

A few days later, two unnamed Flying Squad officers went down to Brentwood in Essex and confronted Det. Inspector Larby. They told him that he had better take back his statement about Robson, or there would be trouble. Larby stood his ground. On 23 April 1972, seven weeks after Robson received seven years, an article appeared in the *Sunday People* newspaper. It reported that Larby had been having an affair with the wife of an imprisoned man, doing seven years too, for receiving stolen goods.

★ ★ ★

Meanwhile, the Flying Squad was also carrying out legitimate business. In 1970, there were 1,550 arrests, but in 1971, incidentally the year that Kenneth Drury was Head, this fell to 1,347 arrests, although property worth £5,750,000 was seized, more than five times the total of the year before. In 1972, of which Drury was Head for only the first three months, arrests went down to 1,081, and property seized back from criminals was just over £780,000. Arrests or property returned to rightful owners would never return to earlier peaks. There were massive upheavals going on in the Metropolitan Police, starting in that year with the appointment of Sir Robert Mark as Commissioner. Mark began a full-scale clean-up of both uniform and CID, which as we have seen was much needed. It was also the year in which the corruption in the Flying Squad began to unravel and be exposed, and this would dog the Squad right through to 1978, when the Squad was effectively devolved. The tremors and then seismic shocks of the previous six years had finally cracked the ground open beneath the Sweeney's feet.

The kidnapping of Muriel McKay, on 28 December 1969, would lead to the Flying Squad being called in to help in the capture of her kidnappers and, as would sadly become clear, killers. Mrs McKay was the wife of Alick McKay, Deputy Chairman of the *News of the World*, which closed down in July 2011 due to a phone-hacking scandal. In 1969, Mr McKay was second in command to the then rising media tycoon Rupert Murdoch. Murdoch was in Australia, and in his absence, he lent his Rolls Royce to Mr McKay. This would inadvertently lead to tragedy, for Mr McKay was being watched by two brothers, Arthur and Nizamodeen Hosein.

Arthur had seen Murdoch being interviewed on television and, realising that he was a man of some considerable means, decided to kidnap Murdoch's wife for ransom, and enlisted the help of Nizamodeen, his easily-led younger brother. They followed the Rolls Royce to a large house in Wimbledon, South-west London, but it wasn't Murdoch's home, it was the McKays. They seized Muriel McKay, not realising their mistake, and demanded ransom in sinister phone calls, in which they pretended to be Mafia types. The ransom drops were put under surveillance, and Flying Squad officers were detailed to this task and others. The Flying Squad would make the arrests of the Hosein brothers in February 1970. One of the officers was Det. Inspector John Bland, whom Jimmy Humphreys would later accuse of allegedly accepting £3,000 from him, according to the Metropolitan Police files. Muriel McKay's body was never found, despite extensive searches. The widely accepted theory was that her body was fed to the pigs kept on the farm by the Hoseins, but this has never been proved.

But the main focus of the Flying Squad was still armed robbery, of course, although it would also have to deal with IRA attacks. A specific incident was what became known as the 'Balcombe Street Siege' in Marylebone in November 1975. IRA terrorists threw a bomb through an exclusive restaurant's window in Mayfair and killed one and injured many. The terrorists were chased by car whilst firing their guns and then on foot by Flying Squad officers, before escaping to Balcombe Street. There they took two people hostage for six days, before surrendering when the SAS were in position.

This was the period immortalised in *The Sweeney* television show, with the stars John Thaw and Dennis Waterman driving, or being driven in, Mark II Jags and souped-up Ford Granadas. 'We're the Sweeney, son, and we haven't 'ad any dinner,' as Thaw's Det. Inspector Regan famously told a 'slag' in one episode. The tone of *The Sweeney* would be fondly revived in the new millennium with the very popular TV show *Life On Mars,* in which a policeman wakes up in the 1970s attached to an unreconstructed, pre-Police and Criminal Evidence Act police unit. It was a time ripe for corruption and police brutality. If an officer was so inclined, as 'Tanky' Challenor has already made clear. This author interviewed ex-Met Police Det. Inspector Andrew Gorzynski, who began his police career in the mid 1970s, and when asked if *The Sweeney* was close to the truth, he said, 'I don't think it was far off the mark.'

The armed robber John McVicar, who would soon be immortalised by Roger Daltrey of The Who in an eponymous film, had been taken in by the Flying Squad as far back as 1966. McVicar had escaped from an eight-year prison sentence and when chased fired shots at the police from his speeding car. He was recaptured by the Flying Squad, but McVicar assaulted one of its officers in the process. It was not long after Harry Roberts had infamously and callously shot dead three police officers in Shepherd's Bush. Therefore, the authorities were in a harsh frame of mind. Consequently, although he hadn't killed or even shot anyone, McVicar received an additional fifteen years, and another five years were added for the assault. But just eighteen months later, McVicar escaped again from Durham Prison, almost becoming Britain's equivalent to the French armed robber, killer and serial escaper Jacques Mesrine. Mesrine would be immortalised in film too, in 2008 by Vincent Cassel, almost thirty years after he had been shot dead in a police ambush in Porte de Clignancourt, Paris, dying like Bonnie and Clyde forty-four years earlier. But unlike Mesrine, McVicar wasn't killed by the Flying Squad when they recaptured him again in November 1970, although both the arresting officers were armed.

Serious robbery was on the rise, and would continue to do so into the early 1980s. The methods of some armed robbers of the 1970s were also imaginative. A former associate of the Richardsons, Jimmy Moody, was part of a crew dubbed the 'Chainsaw Gang', as they cut through security vans using chainsaws, instead of by means of explosives. Moody was caught, but escaped from prison in 1980, and later became a hit-man for hire, until a contract was taken out on him in turn. Moody was shot dead in June 1993. Then there was George Davies, the bank robber who went to prison for raiding the Ilford offices of the London Electricity Board in March 1975.

But Davies' conviction was quashed and he was freed, after a huge miscarriage of justice campaign by his friends and family, which became nationally prominent. Then Davies was caught robbing a branch of the Bank of Cyprus in north London in September 1977 by the Flying Squad, and went back to prison. An unfortunate side effect of the Davies case was that it made it harder to gain public momentum for genuine miscarriages, such as Kenneth Drury's malicious deeds in the Luton Post Office Murder, then still very much ongoing. But the Flying Squad, the Robbery Squad and Regional Crime Squad 9, which were all centrally commanded after 1973 and the shakeup at New Scotland Yard, were obviously pleased to have Davies back behind bars.

The biggest armed robbery of the 1970s was the Bank of America job of 24 April 1975. The enormous sum of more, possibly much more, than £8 million in cash, gems and jewels, as well as antiques of very famous provenance, were taken. This haul was amazingly achieved by plundering less than a fifth of the safety deposit boxes on offer at the branch in Davies Street, Mayfair, and tying up the bank's administrative staff. Less than £500,000 of the Bank of America haul was ever recovered. The inside man was Stuart Buckley, who had a minor criminal record for handling stolen goods. Despite this, Buckley had incredibly worked at the bank as an electrician since January 1975. He had used this access to spy on the bank vaults being opened to get the combinations. Buckley also possessed a detailed knowledge of the bank's electronic systems, as he had helped to redesign them. The main gang was made up of Billy Gear (the lookout), Jimmy O'Loughlin, Peter Colson (the planner), Henry Taylor, Micky 'Skinny' Gervaise (alarms), Henry Jeffrey and Leonard 'Johnny the Bosch' Wilde (the safe-cracker).

The Flying Squad was involved from the start, under the guidance of then Head Det. Chief Supt Jack Slipper, the chaser of Ronnie Biggs. Slipper had found Biggs in Rio de Janeiro, Brazil, in the previous year, but had been unable to have him extradited. Slipper knew that the Bank of America had been a sophisticated job, and he was on the case as soon as the report of the robbery came in from West End Central early next morning. The Flying Squad would bring in Wilde, O'Loughlin and Buckley. The inside man, Buckley, became a 'canary' – a grass – and soon began singing, giving evidence against his criminal associates in return for a lesser sentence.

Det. Supt Bob Robinson, who had helped track down the Great Train Robber Bruce Reynolds in 1968 as a detective sergeant, was put in charge of getting Buckley to sing better. Det. Chief Inspector Mick O'Leary worked alongside Robinson at West End Central. Getting everything out of Buckley would be a lengthy task, but worth it. In November 1976, Wilde would receive twenty-three years and Colson twenty-one years. O'Loughlin, who escaped from court for a short time, but was recaptured, got seventeen years. Henry Jeffrey was given twelve years, Henry Taylor three years. Gervaise got just eighteen months, as he hadn't been involved in restraining the staff and had a very minor previous criminal record. But Gervaise was soon to be a 'supergrass', after being caught with a gang for the robbery of a lorry-load of silver ingots in 1980, in which he wore a policeman's uniform to wave down the lorry. Buckley received seven years, but was released early in January 1978, due to his evidence, provided with a new identity and relocated.

So the Flying Squad was tackling armed gangs throughout the 1970s. With the help of the Robbery Squad and Regional Crime Squad 9, 150 retrospective arrests were made in 1974. Many of these were for lucrative jobs going back to 1965, with twenty-seven convictions resulting, and substantial sentences imposed. Armed robberies in London continued to increase. According to Duncan Campbell in *The Underworld*, there were 380 robberies in 1972 and 1,772 in 1982, a more than four times increase. To give some perspective, the London *Evening Standard* reported in June 2013 that in the year 2008–09 there were 1,270 armed robberies in which a gun was seen or threatened, but by 2012–13, this had fallen to just 514.

The use of informants would always continue – and still does, of course. But after the corruption scandals of 1972–77 involving the Flying, Dirty and Drugs Squads and the necessary castration of the corrupt old CID, followed by the Operation Countryman internal police inquiry of 1978–82, the use of 'snouts' became more tricky for the Metropolitan Police. 'Supergrasses' such as the already mentioned Bertie Smalls and Micky Gervaise, plus Roy Garner, Jimmy Trusty, George Piggott, John Moriarty, et al. were cultivated overtly within the force.

Corrupt senior officers such as Drury, Virgo and Moody would cultivate them covertly, for selfish reasons, and not honest career ones. They would use the need to cultivate informants as a figleaf for corruption. Drury, Moody and Virgo, as well as others, would outwardly, within the Met, nurture relationships with serious criminals to get information for thief-taking or catching pornographers. But this was an excuse for taking bribes, incredible amounts of hospitality, 'drinks' and presents. In return they would turn a blind eye and warn of raids and give other tip-offs. The fact that many in the CID were very territorial about their informants gave those in the elite squads even more autonomy. But in his memoirs, the ex-Commissioner Sir Robert Mark, after his great purge of Metropolitan Police corruption, described the 'informant defence' as a 'highly dubious' one.

So these informants involved in police corruption were not supergrasses, in the sense of the ones mentioned above, who turned Queen's Evidence to gain relative immunity, meaning shorter sentences. These were hardened criminals effectively 'buying' senior officers, and where the senior go, the junior often follow, if they are not wilfully enmeshed and therefore implicated. The fact that the corruption would be linked to Soho and vice can somehow make it seem less serious than if it were murderous gangsters such as the Krays or heavily armed robbers prepared to use firearms.

In actual fact, men such as Bernie Silver, Frank Mifsud and Jimmy Humphreys were dangerous, and feared by others for the threat of violence of which they were thought capable by many. For the outsider, soubriquets such as 'Vice King', 'Porn King', 'Viceroy', and 'Dirty Book Merchant' seem almost devilishly charming and glamorously decadent.

But the reality for Soho insiders was very different. These men were gangsters, and gangsters are predators. Their very survival means gaining and maintaining control by feeding off those lower down the villainous food chain. They would also feed on the police, and the police feed on them, in a mutually beneficial protection–greed relationship. As we know, Jimmy Humphreys was a strip club owner. Along with his previously mentioned interests, he was also running the Big Toe club on Gerrard Street. Humphreys would soon be moving into pornography in a big way too. He was a handsome man, on the make and succeeding, a real man about swinging town by the late 1960s, his wife Rusty very attractive, a golden couple of vice. But Humphreys also had a very dark side, and he was quite capable of using threats of violence, manipulation and frame-ups to achieve his ends. Humphreys' methods would have made his soon-to-be friend Kenneth Drury proud. Humphreys had been a criminal since a very young age and he was streetwise, tough and ruthless.

Murray Goldstein ran several strip clubs in Soho in the late 1960s and early 1970s including Maxim's in Frith Street. His tour de force double act at the club were Jane Martell and David De Santos (stage names), a beautiful blonde woman and a drag artist, for whom Goldstein invented the 'Cage of Lust'. This involved Jane playing an intrepid female explorer and a non-dragged-up David playing a 'jungle boy'. It went down a storm, but to operate his clubs, Goldstein had to deal with what he called his 'police tormentors' on one side, and carnivorous gangsters on the other. In 1967, Humphreys had approached Goldstein with a business proposal, but Goldstein had declined. Goldstein had also run the Big Toe club on Gerrard Street (as a psychedelic-inspired hippy venue), before Humphreys took it over. In his 2005 memoirs *Naked Jungle*, Goldstein recounted another uninvited approach he had from Humphreys in 1969.

This was when Humphreys was about to truly climb up leagues in the Soho hierarchy. His rise would mainly be because of his move into pornography and a business partnership with Bernie Silver of the Syndicate and the 'licensing' of Det. Chief Supt 'Wicked Bill' Moody of the Dirty Squad. Goldstein was in his club 'box-office' in

Rupert Court. Humphreys also had premises on nearby Rupert Street. Goldstein remembered that he was wary of Humphreys when he suddenly appeared, with his henchman, a 'monosyllabic ex-boxer':

> Goldstein: I had heard rumours that he [Humphreys] had become a hard man, an unscrupulous operator who had rivals arrested on trumped-up charges. There was also talk of violence.

Humphreys was friendly when he approached Goldstein, asking if he wanted to have a drink. But it was soon to be confirmed to Goldstein that behind Humphreys's smile, a serpent lurked.

They went to the Round House pub, Goldstein waiting with the henchman while Humphreys got him a half-pint of Carlsberg and himself a Scotch whisky. Then Humphreys asked a seemingly mundane yet menacing question: did Goldstein know that he had been interested in taking on Maxim's, which Goldstein was now making a success? Goldstein had known this, but pretended that he hadn't. Humphreys replied, 'Yes, I was very keen to get it. I was very upset when you took it over. Yeah, I fuckin' was.'

Then Humphreys went in for the kill, to plant the seed of fear in Goldstein's mind. Humphreys said that he had found a key in the cash till when he took over the Big Toe after Goldstein left. Humphreys said that the police had been at the Big Toe recently, and that they had found the key, which had opened a locker at Orly airport in Paris, of all places. And do you know what the police found inside the locker, asked Humphreys? Only machine guns and carbine pistols, that's what. Just before he finished his scotch and left with his henchman, Humphreys said that the police had asked him who had run the Big Toe before him, and that he'd told them. So the police would be paying Goldstein a visit sometime soon, warned Humphreys.

Sure enough, two plain-clothes detectives, from New Scotland Yard no less, not from the local police station West End Central, arrived at Maxim's to see Goldstein a few days later. They knew that Humphreys had told Goldstein to expect them, and they wanted to know about Goldstein's last trip abroad, meaning Paris of course. But Goldstein said that he hadn't been abroad since 1966. The policemen said that they had information that Goldstein had been in Paris in May 1968, incidentally the month of the student revolt, and that the firearms had been left in the locker at Orly airport then. Then the policemen said that they would be back the next day to check Goldstein's passport.

Of course back then all entries into counties were stamped inside passports, so if there was a Paris, France, stamp for 1968, Goldstein was in trouble. That night, Goldstein remembered that he had planned to go to Paris in mid 1968 to buy some sex aids he could sell in London, but had then changed his mind. When the policemen returned, Goldstein could show them that he had not been out of the country for some time, and they left disappointed. But Goldstein did work out how Humphreys had known about the planned trip to Paris: he had told an associate of Humphreys called Bill Keen.

Humphreys had tried to fit up Goldstein to get control of Maxim's. It was ruthless, as if Goldstein had been convicted of possessing and storing firearms, machine guns and carbines no less, he would have faced a serious stretch in prison. There is no way of knowing if those two policemen were in the pay of Humphreys, but it is possible. If they were not, then Humphreys had just tipped them off to get what he wanted. Were the firearms ever in the airport locker? It's possible they were never there, and if the policemen were in league with Humphreys, it could have just been scare tactics to get Goldstein out of Soho.

As well as developing corrupt ties with powerful police officers, it can be said with certainty that Humphreys was a police informer, as has been the underworld view since the 1970s. The Met files show us more detail about this aspect of Humphreys' complex police relationships, and more on this shortly. But first, Humphreys would get into business with Bernie Silver, Det. Chief Supt Moody and another financial beneficiary of his and Silver's illicit enormous police payments, Commander Wally Virgo.

★ ★ ★

The Criterion restaurant, Piccadilly Circus, late December 1969, evening

Attached to the adjacent Criterion Theatre, the restaurant that shares its name serves good-quality food at medium–expensive prices. It isn't the Savoy, Le Caprice, or any of the other very high-end restaurants that Jimmy and Rusty Humphreys frequent, but it's decent and a cut above. There's Jimmy Humphreys, in his expensive suit, hair neither long nor short, and Rusty, a fine-looking woman who knows it very well, her tousled hair framing her pretty features, more intelligent than her husband. They are a great vice team.

And who's that opposite, with the worried face, his already old-world trilby and leather gloves on the table? Why, it's Commander Wally Virgo, Head of Central Office and overall commander of nine elite Metropolitan Police squads. What could he be doing here with Jimmy, who has a criminal record almost as long as Muhammad Ali's arm? And who is that next to Commander Virgo, with the cherubic face? It's only Bernie Silver, joint head of the Syndicate, Soho kingpin, with a huge immoral earnings income and a menacing reputation. What an interesting gathering, almost within echo distance of Soho itself, and not far from Silver's headquarters in Haymarket.

Just over three years ago, in November 1966, the theatre next door started running Joe Orton's play *Loot*, a characteristically black-humoured farce. One of the chief purveyors of that farce was the character Det. Inspector Truscott. Commander Virgo left that rank behind years ago. Orton was cruelly murdered by his lover Kenneth Halliwell in the summer of 1967, but if Joe could have seen this scene – a very senior police officer sitting with two high-profile gangsters and the vice operator wife of one of them – he surely would have laughed darkly and written another farce.

What's Jimmy saying? He's looking serious. He's only complaining … that's what he's doing. What? Det. Chief Supt 'Wicked Bill' Moody, head of the Obscene Publications Squad, won't give him a license to open a dirty bookshop at his Rupert Street premises. Mean old Moody. But surely Moody *should* be trying to close down such establishments under the law, not sanctioning them? Not a bit of it. Moody's superior officer Virgo looks sympathetic. Silver says he will see what he can do. Jimmy and Rusty look at each other and smile. This looks promising.

★ ★ ★

Indeed it was. Shortly after, Det. Chief Supt 'Wicked Bill' Moody and Jimmy Humphreys met in a restaurant in exclusive Mayfair, to iron out a deal. Bernie Silver, already a close associate of Moody, had smoothed the path, and Commander Virgo almost certainly would have put in a good word for Humphreys. Above all, the potential pound signs conjured their magic. But Moody knew his worth, and wanted hard terms. To open his porn bookshop in Rupert Street, Humphreys would have to take Silver as a fifty-fifty partner. Silver was no doubt aware of this being on the table, and due to the lucrative half-share of the profits, was only too happy to oblige. The enormously corrupt Moody trusted Silver, and wanted him involved, as he knew that Silver had real power in Soho. Any trouble could be sorted out by the big man. Humphreys accepted.

Then there was the license. Moody held the cards, and Humphreys was desperate to make the killing he knew selling pornography in Soho would bring him. Various sources have said that the figure was £12,000 or £14,000, but the Met files show that Humphreys said that Moody wanted £10,000 for the license, still enough to buy a row of houses in some parts of London. On top of that, Humphreys would have to pay Moody £2,000 a month for protection, to keep his shop open and prevent police raids. Humphreys agreed to it all.

So, as the 1970s dawned, Jimmy Humphreys finally had his entrée into the porn trade. The cost of that entry was very high, but so would be the profits. Being in partnership with Silver was not ideal in some ways, as Humphreys would always be the junior partner. But Silver's power would immediately give Humphreys more power too, making him a leading Soho face. Humphreys' deal with the feared Moody would also give him clout. It's no wonder that the gangster 'Mad' Frankie Fraser once said that the police had 'a licence' to do what they wanted in 1950s and 1960s Soho. In a little while, Humphreys would also add the Head of the Flying Squad, Kenneth Drury, to his list of corrupt police friends too.

★ ★ ★

Less than three weeks after Det. Chief Supt Kenneth Drury had seen his venal fit-up of Murphy, Cooper and McMahon for the Luton Post Office Murder pay off, he was rewarded. Drury was handpicked to investigate a very sensitive case in Northern Ireland. The closing of the investigation into the murder of Reginald Stevens with then unknown virulently unsafe convictions had undoubtedly improved Drury's stock within the Metropolitan Police. Whoever said that crime doesn't pay?

The case which Drury was designated to investigate had resulted in a man's death. That man, Samuel Devenny, is widely considered to be the first victim of the Troubles in Northern Ireland, the 'war' between the IRA and the British State, with the Loyalists theoretically on the side of the latter. On 19 April 1969, there had been a riot in Derry, and Devenny and others in his family were allegedly attacked by members of the Royal Ulster Constabulary (RUC), the then police force of Northern Ireland. The RUC would later be accused of terrible collusion and obstruction of justice in later sectarian murders. These included that of the Loyalist paramilitary leader Billy Wright, and the Republican human rights lawyers Patrick Finucane and Rosemary Nelson. (This author also co-wrote a book about Rosemary Nelson's murder.)

Sammy Devenny died almost three months to the day of the attack, on 17 July 1969, his family saying that he had never recovered from his injuries. There had already been an internal investigation by the RUC after a complaint made by the Devenny family's lawyer. For obvious reasons this was not deemed to be sufficient. Therefore, the Chief Constable of the RUC, Sir Arthur Young, asked the Met for assistance, and Det. Chief Supt Drury was appointed. Drury's task was to lead an independent inquiry into Devenny's death and its causes. Drury was to be assisted by Det. Sgt Churchill-Coleman, and they arrived in Northern Ireland on 6 April 1970. It was a very important investigation, and copies of Drury's final report would go to the Chief Constable of the RUC, and the Prime Minister and Attorney General of Northern Ireland. Drury was obviously seen as a trusted and resourceful police officer, and a safe pair of hands.

In his final report, Drury concluded that it was impossible to establish which RUC officers had participated in the attack on Devenny, but that up to eight officers could have been involved. He also reported that he could not conclusively say from the medical evidence if Devenny's death had been as a result of the injuries he had suffered in the attack three months earlier. Drury was also critical of the RUC's internal investigation, and his words leave no doubt that he felt that RUC officers had been involved in the attack.

> Drury: Whilst it is appreciated that officers of the force [RUC] on duty in the riot area on the day in question were under extreme provocation … there is no evidence that their action … could be justified in any way and this code of conduct can never be condoned in any force responsible for the preservation of law and order.

A worthy statement if it had come from a senior police officer of integrity. But in actual fact, Drury's investigation into Sammy Devenny's death and allegations of RUC involvement in the attack was given a clean bill of health by the Police Ombudsman in 2001. Incredibly, the Devenny family had not had access to Drury's report in 1970 or since, until thirty-one years later. Now they were able to see the report, and the Ombudsman upheld their complaint against the RUC.

This new but long overdue transparency obviously had a great deal to do with the RUC being disbanded and the Police Service Northern Ireland (PSNI) replacing it at this time. Regarding the quality of Det. Chief Supt Drury's investigation, the 2001 inquiry stated: 'The Police Ombudsman concludes from the examination of the Drury Report that the investigation he carried out, in contrast to the internal investigation by the RUC, was extensive and thorough.'

On returning from Northern Ireland, Drury went back to the Murder Squad. But on 2 November 1970 he was transferred to the Flying Squad, where he had served for a year fifteen years earlier. For the next two months, Drury acted as Deputy Head of the Squad under Commander Frank 'Jeepers' Davies. Within a few years, Davies, who had an MBE, would inexplicably give evidence on behalf of the Soho ponce and joint head of Soho's Syndicate, Bernie Silver, at his trial. Drury wasn't to be number two for long though. At Christmas 1970, less than two months after he returned to the Flying Squad, Davies retired from the Metropolitan Police. Detective Chief Superintendent Kenneth Drury became Head of the Flying Squad on 1 January 1971.

This was a steep rise, and it had obviously been brought about by Drury's unbelievably corrupt clean-up of the Luton Post Office Murder, and his Northern Ireland assignment, which he had handled satisfactorily. On 12 April 1971, almost twenty-five years after he joined the Metropolitan Police, Drury was made a Commander, the same rank as the greedily corrupt Wally Virgo, diner with gangsters. But Drury would soon be putting Virgo to shame. No Criterion restaurant for Drury, only the very best.

It was sometime in 1971 that Drury met Jimmy Humphreys, the man whose criminal file he had drawn thirty years earlier when he was a detective constable on 'L' Division. They met at a party that Humphreys gave to celebrate the promotion of another Flying Squad member, whose identity cannot be ascertained. But this does prove that Humphreys had at least one close contact inside the Flying Squad before he became chums with Drury. As the Met files show, Humphreys said in a later police statement that very early in their 'association', he gave Drury a 'drink' of £50.

> Humphreys, in his statement: It was the custom in the West End. It was a token of friendship of a form. I wanted him as a friend in case he could help me. In the West End you could get involved. He was the head of the Flying Squad and could be a useful friend.

Later, Humphreys would claim that he put Drury on a retainer of £100 a week for a time. Drury's salary as Head of the Flying Squad was a good one for the early 1970s, £4,600 a year. That works out at £88.50 a week, so for a period Humphreys more than doubled Drury's salary, and over half of Drury's income, legal and illicit, came from Soho's 'Porn King'. In the same police statement, Humphreys explained why he had paid Drury so much money weekly: 'As I have said, he was a useful friend, and it kept the Flying Squad away from the porn business.' Soho was not the usual focus of the Flying Squad, but the criminals it chased were often to be found in the area, and Humphreys was ensuring that he would get no heat from the Flying Squad. What he did not mention was that he was also buying huge police influence from a senior officer in charge of an elite squad, and that was very worthwhile. Humphreys was also acting as a police informer for Drury specifically on occasion.

Humphreys was by now of course raking in the profits, and using his expensive police contacts to manipulate other vice operators and stay on top. But his new partnership with the far more powerful Bernie Silver was now under some strain. Silver was abroad for a spell in 1971, and Humphreys did something very unwise. Silver's long-term girlfriend was Dominique Ferguson, and while Silver was out of the country, Humphreys had a fling with her. Silver knew everything that happened in Soho, and when he came back, quickly found out. This was personal. James Morton points out in *Gangland Soho* that Silver had a discussion with a senior detective whilst on a day out at Sandown racecourse, and the gist of the conversation was about how they could fit-up Humphreys. In fact, Humphreys was probably lucky that his corpse wasn't found in Epping Forest, or at least didn't get a good slashing or going-over.

It was his new friend Drury to whom Humphreys turned when he heard on the grapevine that Silver was going to have him fitted up in revenge. This of course made Humphreys extremely anxious, as he knew that Silver had serious power in the Metropolitan Police through his extensive associations with policemen of all ranks. Just like Humphreys had tried to do to Murray Goldstein in 1969, Silver could do to him, and worse. Drury went and spoke to Silver on behalf of Humphreys, and soon it was all sorted out. It is not known what calmed Silver down, whether Humphreys had to pay Silver money or increase the share of porn profits he gave to Silver. But what was Drury's fee for this mediation service between two high-profile Soho gangsters, a ponce and a pornographer? According to Humphreys, he gave Drury £1,050 for his help in this desperate instance, an unrounded figure. One can imagine that the £50 was the preliminary 'drink' when Drury agreed to help, and the remaining £1,000 paid when Silver had been placated by Drury and Humphreys could breathe again.

The relationship between Drury and Humphreys became a close one socially, as we will shortly see. In his memoirs, Joey Pyle remembered that he often saw Drury at Humphreys' home, and that it was 'no secret amongst the chaps', meaning his fellow underworld friends. It was a relationship which was financially very profitable for Drury, as well as having many other perks, and Humphreys had a powerful police ally. Already involved with Det. Chief Supt Moody, Head of the Dirty Squad, and Commander Virgo, Head of Central Office, he now had the Head of the Sweeney under his patronage. Jimmy had got into bed with Wicked Bill, Wally and Ken, and they were mutually pleasing and profitable friendships. But they were also dangerous ones.

It was the *Sunday People* newspaper (it had changed its name from the *People*) that began to probe into Metropolitan Police corruption. The paper's investigations editor, Laurie Manifold, was the driving force behind it. Manifold had joined the *People* in 1950, at the very time when Duncan Webb was exposing the vice kings the Messinas in the paper, later serialising his friend Billy Hill's memoirs. Manifold would follow in Webb's footsteps as the paper's investigations tsar, and after a spell on the *Daily Sketch*, he returned to the *People* as News Editor. It was his exposure of a 1964 football gambling scandal, as a result of which footballers were jailed, which really made his name as an investigative journalist. Manifold would use undercover and covert techniques to get his evidence. In the mid 1960s, the *People*, published every Sunday, had a circulation of more than five and a half million, but by 1970 this was in decline. By then, Laurie Manifold was the Assistant Editor of the paper.

In 1971–72, Manifold and the *Sunday People* were focusing on pornography. It was a bête noire for the public; British society was widely regarded as becoming too permissive. Lord Longford, future champion of the Moors Murderer Myra Hindley, was carrying out a self-financed investigation into the evils of pornography of his own, for instance. Manifold's team later calculated, in an article of 6 February 1972, that approximately 2 million dirty magazines had been sold, and that 300,000 'blue movies' were projected in 1971. Pornographic films were the specialism of the 'blue movie kings' 'Big' Jeff Phillips and Gerald Citron, who both lived in mansions in Esher, Surrey, although Phillips had several properties.

For the first time, the *Sunday People* named Soho vice operators such as Bernie Silver, 'Big Frank' Mifsud, Jimmy Humphreys and John 'Eric' Mason (who ran ten shops and clubs). In August 1971 *The Observer* and the satirical campaigning magazine *Private Eye* reported on police corruption in Soho, but neither was able to give the names of individuals involved. The year 1972 was when corruption in the Flying Squad began to be truly exposed in the newspapers. In late February, it was Laurie Manifold who pricked Commander Kenneth Drury's corrupt bubble at last. As we now know, the gangster Joey Pyle passed information to a journalist, who in turn gave it to Manifold.

In politics, the Troubles in Northern Ireland reached new levels of dangerous gravity on 'Bloody Sunday', when British soldiers shot dead thirteen protesters in Derry in January 1972, the city where Sammy Devenny had lived and Drury investigated his death. By February, a miner's strike in Britain caused power cuts to be ordered by Edward Heath's Conservative government. Drury might have wished that would stop the printing presses of the *Sunday People*, but it was not to be.

4

ROTTEN FROM THE OUTSIDE IN

Sunday People, 27 February 1972

POLICE CHIEF AND THE 'PORN' KING

**A grave question in the public interest
Was it wise for Commander Drury of the Yard
to go on holiday with this old lag?**

*by Laurie Manifold, head of the team of Sunday People
reporters investigating pornography in Britain*

THE HEAD of Scotland Yard's world-famous Flying Squad has just been spending an expensive holiday abroad with one of Britain's most notorious pornographers- a man with an appalling criminal record.

Commander Kenneth Drury, 49, and wife, with 'dirty' bookshop tycoon James William Humphreys, 42, and wife, were together for a fortnight, partly in Cyprus, partly in the Lebanon...

It was a long article, and was of course damaging, as millions of people read it over the course of that late winter Sunday. Manifold credited Drury with having twenty-three police commendations. This figure would be repeated by other contemporary journalists, and many other sources since have reported that number. But Drury's service record in the Met files shows that he actually had thirteen major commendations and no minor ones. But when the article called Drury 'one of the most prominent and powerful officers in London', this was undoubtedly true. Humphreys had been investigated in detail, and his company, Humphreys Entertainments Ltd, had come under the close scrutiny of Manifold and his team of reporters.

Manifold also stated in the article that he had passed the information in the article to New Scotland Yard the week before. Manifold had then been called in and interviewed for an hour by Deputy Assistant Commissioner Richard Chitty and none other than Commander Wally Virgo, patron of the Criterion restaurant with Humphreys and Silver. At that interview, Manifold asked to speak to the Metropolitan Police Commissioner Sir John Waldron and directly to Drury. Both requests were denied.

Also, on pages three and four of that day's *Sunday People*, police corruption was highlighted by Manifold and his team. So although the article about Drury and Humphreys did not overtly allege corruption on Drury's part, anybody reading the first four pages of that day's paper was in no doubt that certain, as yet unnamed, officers were being accused of having their noses in the Soho trough. On page three, the headline was 'Corruption – The Charges Against the Police'. Page three had 'Bookshop Owners Pay £1,000 a Week to the Police', and this information had come from 'Lord Longford's private eye'. As already mentioned, Longford was conducting his own crusading investigation into pornography. The first article included an interview with the American pornographer Charles Julian, who operated in Soho. Julian had previous convictions for 'handling' porn, burglary and possession of drugs at this time. He was an associate of Soho blue movie king 'Big' Jeff Phillips, and it was in Phillips' company that Julian had witnessed police wrongdoing.

On two separate occasions, Julian had been with Phillips at the exclusive Inn on the Park hotel along with a man Phillips said was 'an officer of the Obscene Publications Department at Scotland Yard'. Julian said that Phillips had given an envelope full of cash to the Dirty Squad officer. Julian had also been at a dinner at one of Phillips' homes in Wargrave, Berkshire, when the same officer was there along with his wife and children, hosted by Phillips and his wife. Finally, he had been at a party at Phillips' flat in Sloane Square, Chelsea, and a different Dirty Squad officer was there. Phillips had thoughtfully supplied hostesses for entertainment. According to Julian, 'There were two bedrooms, and we all took turns in using them with girls.'

With the aid of the Metropolitan Police files, the full details of Drury's corruption with Humphreys and how other members of the Flying Squad and the Dirty Squad became implicated can be told for the first time. The whole story of the police investigations, which would continue until 1976-77, including key statements, can be revealed.

The Metropolitan Police appointed Deputy Assistant Commissioner Sheppard of the No. 1 Inspectorate to 'investigate the alleged improper relationship' between Drury and Humphreys. This appointment was made on Friday 25 February 1972, two days before the article appeared, and obviously in response to Manifold's interview with Chitty and Virgo, which had taken place on Thursday 24 February. Manifold was then called back in for two interviews on Tuesday 29 February, and his junior reporter Sydney Foxcroft would also be interviewed on 7 March. Both Manifold and Foxcroft would make clear that they were not alleging corruption (they could not prove it yet). Both journalists explained that the public interest for the story was the 'undesirable social association' between the Head of the Flying Squad and a prominent pornographer. Manifold said that he could supply information proving that Humphreys was involved in pornography, but Foxcroft could not. Manifold was interviewed by DAC Fred Sheppard, and Det. Chief Supt Tommy Morrison, who was Commander Drury's second-in-command in the Flying Squad.

Manifold refused to name his source for the Drury–Humphreys holiday story, saying, 'A journalist, as a matter of principle, never discloses his sources of information.' It is known that Joey Pyle was the original source, but he did not inform Manifold directly. Another journalist passed the information on. But as already mentioned, Drury would make an allegation against that journalist for looking into him in 1971 about Patrick Murphy's unsafe conviction in the Luton Post Office Murder. As this journalist could not be traced by the author, it would be unethical to name him here. Manifold declined to make a formal statement, unless it was a requirement of legal or disciplinary proceedings, which at this stage it was not.

But the transcripts of the 29 February interviews are in the Met files and do offer a few interesting facts. Manifold had interviewed Jimmy Humphreys on three occasions, the last time being on 25 February 1972, when he asked Humphreys about the holiday with Drury and their wives, Joan Drury and June 'Rusty' Humphreys. Manifold told DAC Sheppard and Det. Chief Supt Morrison, 'Humphreys confirmed the holiday and said he very much regretted that I had got hold of it.'

Humphreys confirmed that the holiday had taken place because he had no choice. But most interesting were Manifold's comments about Humphreys admitting to him that he had been a police informant. Humphreys had told him that he 'had given considerable help to the police … in particular he had helped the police with information about the Reading murder.' This reference to a murder in Reading, Berkshire, and Humphreys acting as a police informant in relation to it was also mentioned by both Humphreys and Drury in their police statements. The Metropolitan Police was taking the revelations about Drury very seriously, and a full-scale internal inquiry was taking place. This would involve many interviews, with the protagonists, an assortment of police officers of various ranks, and those who were involved in selling the holiday at the travel agents.

Jimmy Humphreys was interviewed by Sheppard and Morrison on 1 March 1972. Under the instructions of his lawyer Michael Lawson, he didn't respond to any questions, but he did give statements on 1 March and 3 March. In both statements, Humphreys gave his address as 13–14 Dean Street, Soho. Humphreys:

> On January 14 1972 I went for two weeks to Cyprus together with my wife, Commander Kenneth Drury and his wife. I made the arrangements for the trip, Commander Drury paid me for his wife's and his own share

and I arranged payment to the travel agents who were [Thomas] Cooks. I had reason to believe that Ronald Biggs would be there.'

This was the first mention of Ronnie Biggs, the Great Train Robber. He was still on the run abroad after escaping from prison – despite repeated attempts by the Metropolitan Police, in the form of investigations led by Tommy Butler and Leonard 'Nipper' Read, to locate him and bring him back.

As would later emerge, the idea that Humphreys and Drury were in Cyprus to find Biggs had been cooked up between them after the publication of the newspaper article on 27 February and before Humphreys' first statement, a matter of a few days. Or probably since Manifold had approached Humphreys with the information he had on 25 February. Humphreys said that they had flown to Famagusta in Cyprus and that they were 'given to understand' that Biggs was in Beirut, just a thirty-minute flight away, so they had gone to Beirut. Drury paid for this Lebanese excursion, according to Humphreys, who also stressed, 'I had never been on holiday with Commander Drury or his wife before.'

Humphreys also confirmed another allegation made by Manifold in his article. He had been at the Annual Dinner of the Flying Squad at the exclusive Grosvenor House Hotel in October 1971. But Humphreys said that he was 'not a guest of or in any way invited by Commander Drury. I was the guest of another party who paid for me.' The identity of this person is unknown, but of course Humphreys had high-ranking police contacts other than Drury.

Bernie Silver also attended that dinner and others, and it almost beggars belief that hardened criminals such as them were at the Flying Squad's official yearly function. But then Silver and Humphreys also attended boxing events arranged by the Soho gym owner Jack Solomon at the Grosvenor House Hotel too. That is not to forget that Humphreys and Drury had first met at a party Humphreys held for another Flying Squad officer. So the connections between the Flying Squad and the Soho underworld were obviously firmly established.

Humphreys then reminded the police that he had been helpful to them as an informant. This would be echoed by Drury in his statement, being the central argument in defence of his association with Humphreys: 'I have assisted police officers in the past and in particular I gave information to Commander Drury which led to the arrest of a man who was eventually convicted of the murder of a police detective in Reading.' This was the same case which Humphreys had mentioned to Manifold.

It was the murder of Det. Constable Ian Coward in June 1971 in Reading. Coward had seen a car being driven dangerously and stopped it. As he was radioing for back-up, two men got out of the car and shot DC Coward nine times. The car was stolen and had just been used to steal firearms and ammunition. Coward struggled on for almost a month, but then died of his injuries. In December 1971, Coward posthumously received the Queen's Police Medal (QPM). In the same month, Coward's killers, Arthur Skingle and Peter Sparrow, were caught and later convicted. Skingle died in prison in 1987, and Sparrow was released in 1994.

As we will see from Drury's statement, it was Skingle about whom Humphreys supplied information to the police, allowing the Flying Squad to arrest him. At the end of his first statement, there is a note added in Humphreys' own handwriting, followed by his signature: 'I have never been to Cyprus before and I have never been to Greece. Mr Drury has never stayed or had the use of any villa of mine in Spain.' In his second statement two days later, Humphreys added more detail, saying that Drury had repaid the money he had outlaid for their holiday at the travel agents: 'It was paid to me in cash shortly after the travel agents had been paid. Mr Drury had insisted on seeing that I had paid before he paid me.'

There was also the issue of the receipt at the travel agents, which had stated Drury's address as 55 Rupert Street, London W1. The Met files show that the premises consisted of 'a ground floor shop selling pornographic literature, with a flat above'. Also, that the coin box telephone there had been rented by Humphreys, trading as 'R.A. Hustler', and giving his occupation as 'Corn Dealer'. This shows that this leading porn dealer had a sense of humour. This was the address in Soho where Humphreys had opened his porn bookshop in partnership with Silver, with the help of Det. Chief Supt Moody's expensive license and monthly retainer. Drury, his wife Joan and their three children, two daughters and a son, lived in Sidcup, Kent. Humphreys gave his reasons why he had given a false address for Drury: 'Firstly I thought he would prefer it if I tried to keep the trip as secret as possible and secondly I did not know his address.'

Humphreys concluded his second statement by saying that in his view, the *People* article of 27 February was 'highly inaccurate and defamatory of myself and of Commander Drury'. He had received legal counsel and a 'Letter before Action' libel writ against both the newspaper and Laurie Manifold. This was never followed up of course, as Manifold's article was all true.

The media were on fire about the story now. Two other newspapers had got wind of Manifold's scoop, and had published shorter articles on the same day. The *Sunday Express* went with 'Inquiry Into Yard Chief's Holiday' and Ron Mount of the *News of the World* ran 'Why Yard Chief Holidayed With Porn Boss'. Mount had interviewed Humphreys at his 'luxury flat' and Humphreys told him about the search for Biggs in Cyprus and Beirut after a tip-off. It is surprising that Humphreys was so prepared to admit this so publicly. It meant that he was helping the Head of the Flying Squad track down another extremely high-profile criminal, therefore making him a 'grass', a breed detested by the underworld.

Then on 28 February, Drury himself had given an interview to Leslie Hinton of the *Sun*, which appeared as 'Yard Boss: I'm Innocent' and in which Drury called Humphreys 'an acquaintance'. Drury added that he was not worried about the investigation. 'I have done nothing to reproach myself for,' said Drury. But Drury added that he was concerned about the effect on his family, and that his wife was very upset by all the publicity. On the same day, the *Daily Mirror* had 'My Holiday With Strip King' and the *Daily Mail's* Peter Burden ran 'I Paid For My Trip – Yard Chief'. It was against Metropolitan Police rules for officers to speak to the media about investigations involving themselves. This would also be held against Drury, especially as he continued to give newspaper interviews in the next weeks, as well as to television and radio. Drury, and for some reason, Humphreys, out of loyalty to Drury or more likely to protect his police network, were attempting damage limitation. They were obviously hoping that the Biggs motive for the holiday would become the received view.

Commander Wally Virgo was also attracting media interest. In March 1972, the *News of the World* contacted him and said that they were going to publish a story about him. The gist of it was the allegation that Virgo and his wife had gone on holiday to Ireland with Bernie Silver, Virgo's dining partner at the Criterion restaurant in December 1969. It was alleged that Silver had paid for the holiday. Virgo would later claim that he immediately contacted the Met Police Commissioner John Waldron about the matter. The story never appeared, and the corrupt Virgo was outraged that the *News of the World* never apologised to him. Meanwhile, regarding the Drury–Humphreys holiday, the No. 1 Area Inspectorate had also interviewed the staff of the Thomas Cook travel agents in Oxford Street. This was a short walk from Humphreys' Soho base, and the Met files show copies of the receipts issued to Humphreys.

Humphreys booked a holiday for four to Famagusta, Cyprus, to depart on 14 January and return on 28 January 1972. The booking was made with a £25 deposit paid in cash on 1 December 1971, and the £488 balance was paid by cheque on 8 December. Humphreys had also bought £500 worth of traveller's cheques on 13 January, the day before the holiday began. Most strange though was the fact that the March 1972 police investigation had discovered that a man had returned to the Thomas Cook travel agents on 25 February 1972. This was almost a month after the holiday had finished, and the day on which Manifold had interviewed Humphreys and informed him what he knew about the holiday. The man gave his name as 'James Humphreys' to a member of the travel agency staff, and told him that he had recently come back from holiday in Cyprus. He had then asked for confirmation of the amounts he had paid, for tax purposes. Not questioning the man's identity, the travel agent clerk had produced the receipt, but the man had said that not all of the names were on it. Neither Kenneth nor Joan Drury was listed. The man asked for them to be added, which they were.

The Met files show that after the police investigators spoke to the clerk, he was eventually able to identify the man who had posed as Humphreys as 'Mark Oliver'. Oliver was an ex-constable in the Metropolitan Police, who had last served more than twenty-five years earlier, in June 1946. Coincidentally, this was the very month in which Drury had joined the Metropolitan Police. The implication clearly is that after Manifold spoke to Humphreys, either Humphreys or Drury sent Oliver around to the travel agent to get the names of Drury and his wife added. In his statement of 3 March, Humphreys said 'I have not been in contact with [Thomas] Cook's in any way since the trip.' This is probably true, as Oliver had apparently visited on their behalf. Drury knew that if he had in any way seemed to be covering his tracks about the holiday, he would look guiltier. Drury's very brazenness played right into his forthcoming defence that he was merely cultivating Humphreys as an informant.

The fact that Jimmy Humphreys had attended the annual Flying Squad dinner at the Grosvenor House Hotel on Park Lane on 5 October 1971 was being investigated too. The press had also been vigorously trying to access photographs of the dinner, which had had 900 guests. Det. Sgt Peter Jones was a member of the Flying Squad and also the Assistant Social Secretary of the Flying Squad Athletic Club, which organised the annual dinner. Det. Sgt Jones gave a statement to No. 1 Area Inspectorate on 2 March 1972. This related mainly to the photographs which had been taken at the dinner, by a firm called Synchroflash. It had been contracted to take official photographs at the hotel's functions, under the name of the Grosvenor House Photographic Service.

On 28 February, the day after the *People* article appeared, Jones had taken a call from the Fleet Street News Agency: 'We want photographs of Commander Drury and Mr Humphreys taken at the Flying Squad dinner.' Of course, such a controversial picture would have been tabloid gold. Jones had said that the news agency 'could demand nothing from me' and they could come to New Scotland Yard to speak to him directly if they wished. The caller hung up. Immediately, the phone rang again, and it was the manager of Synchroflash, saying that both the news agency and somebody from the *Sunday People* had asked him for copies of any photographs with Drury and Humphreys in them. Jones had told the manager not to supply them under any circumstances, and to contact him if there were any more problems. The media was scenting blood now and circling.

At the same time, the No. 1 Area Inspectorate was busy taking statements from police officers regarding Commander Drury, and of course, any knowledge they had about Humphreys. Regarding Humphreys, it's also interesting to note that a separate entry in the Met files records a visit Jimmy Humphreys had made to New Scotland Yard around fifteen months earlier, on 18 December 1969. This was at the very time that Humphreys was going into business with Det. Chief Supt 'Wicked Bill' Moody and Bernie Silver. Not to forget that Commander Virgo also benefitted very nicely from this arrangement, as would later come out.

There is no way of knowing for sure why Humphreys was there, but he was being questioned about the Soho underworld, and the police had a view. A police opinion is given at the end of the entry. It reads: 'Not a truthful man. Hiding his own activities. Formed the opinion that he only came to New Scotland Yard in endeavour to find out lines of enquiry.' That this opinion was held in late 1969 implicates the dishonesty displayed by members of the Dirty Squad less than three years later. Those Dirty Squad officers, who were of course supposed to be Humphreys' nemesis, said that they had no knowledge of his pornography activities in March 1972. At this time, many crime reporters in Fleet Street already knew about Humphreys' porn activities.

On that December 1969 visit, Humphreys had admitted owning leases at 37 Berwick Street, and what he called his 'hardware' shop at 55 Rupert Street. This was soon to be the site of his and Silver's porn shop, sanctioned by Moody. Humphreys also said that he ran bookshops at 6 Walker's Court and 17 D'Arblay Street. The New Hogarth Club was located on D'Arblay Street too, where Humphreys would later sometimes meet Drury. Humphreys told the police that Silver and 'Big Frank' Mifsud were partners in properties, but that he had no knowledge of who was 'controlling girls'. It was mainly Silver and Mifsud, of course, but saying anything about their poncing and pimping activities would have been very bad for Jimmy's health. He also said that he had no idea if the two heads of the Syndicate had any interests in bookshops and strip clubs, another understandable lie.

But he did say that Silver was connected to Victor Micallef, another prominent Syndicate figure. Humphreys also said, to quote the police, that he knew all the 'infamous people in the West End, but says he keeps himself to himself and does not mix with any of them socially'. The most outrageous thing reported was that Humphreys said he 'does not know any policemen who mix with West End characters'. At a time when Humphreys was having dinner at the Criterion with Commander Virgo and in a Mayfair restaurant with Det. Chief Supt Moody, this was patently untrue. Not only did he know that policemen were mixing with underworld figures, but he had spun his own corrupt web with them too.

Fast forward to March 1972, and let's see what members of the Dirty Squad told the No. 1 Area Inspectorate about Humphreys. In a statement dated 8 March, Det. Chief Supt Eric Payton, who had been in the Dirty Squad for eighteen months, and had recently taken over as Head said, 'I have been asked if I have any knowledge of James Humphreys being engaged in importing, dealing or trading in pornographic materials. I have no such knowledge, and he has never been reported to me as so engaged.'

Det. Chief Inspector Henry Robertson had been in the Dirty Squad for just three months. On 9 March he said that he had searched Humphreys' premises at 37 Berwick Street when attached to a different unit in 1969. He thought that the club on that site, the Queen's, was owned by Humphreys, as it was. But Robertson also said, 'Since I have been engaged on the Obscene Publications Squad, to date, I have received no information that James Humphreys is connected in any way in the distribution, or dealing with pornographic material.' At this time, Humphreys was one of the biggest pornography importers and dealers in Soho, and was widely known as such. Manifold had called Humphreys 'one of Britain's most notorious pornographers' in his *People* article, just ten days before these statements were made.

Det. Chief Supt Eric Pitts had been attached to the Vine Street sub-division of the Dirty Squad from October to December 1970. Since 1 January 1971, Pitts was in charge of 'C' Division Clubs Office, which dealt with the supervision and licensing enquiries of registered clubs and the detection and suppression of brothels, disorderly houses, persons living on immoral earnings, licensed gaming premises and unlicensed betting and lotteries. In a lengthy statement on 11 March 1972, Pitts explained that prior to 1967 such clubs operated in Soho were called 'strip clubs'. After 1967 they had become known as 'strip theatres' when licensing began.

Pitts said that:

> There is no regular system of visits to these or other premises. Infrequent visits are made to ensure that the performances are within the bounds of decency and are not of an obscene nature. Generally any objectionable performances would be learned by way of information received.

Just four clubs had been prosecuted as disorderly houses since licensing came into force. It's also enlightening to see why men such as Jimmy Humphreys opened 'booking offices' for their clubs. These premises had previously been strip clubs, but when licensing came in, they had not been granted a license due to being structurally unsuitable.

The statement is also interesting on how porn bookshops were policed.

> Pitts: Where books are displayed in windows and on view to the public, which have covers which are considered to offend against decency, the person in charge of the premises, and who so placed the books on view, normally a shop manager or other employee, is dealt with by way of arrest or summons for the offence of 'wilfully exposing to view' an obscene print, picture or other indecent exhibition.

The list of those arrested or summonsed, thirty since 1 January 1971, so fourteen months, shows no leading Soho names. One person named was just 16 years old and obviously a dogsbody. As Pitts related, it was the person on the premises at the time who was prosecuted, not the owner or supplier of the pornography. This was how Humphreys had never been pulled in for pornography, along with the fact that he was being protected by Moody, Virgo and Drury, a detective chief superintendent and two commanders. Humphreys also had corrupt links to other more junior officers too.

Humphreys' most prominent Soho interests included the Queen's Theatre Strip Club at 37 Berwick Street and the Queen's booking office at 5 Walker's Court and the adjacent bookshop. Humphreys was the rateable occupier of that bookshop in 1965, but since 1966 it was under another name. Then there was the bookshop at 55 Rupert Street which Humphreys ran in partnership with Silver and his corrupt police friends and the Sandra East X Boutique at 19 Wardour Street. Rusty Humphreys was one of the three proprietors of the Sandra East X Boutique. Other sex boutiques had also been operated at 58 Greek Street and 53 Shepherds Market, but had since closed since the Sandra East X Boutique was prosecuted for selling 'poisons'. The premises at 58 Greek Street had previously been owned by Selim Mehmet, and Humphreys had bought it from him in 1970. We will be meeting Selim Mehmet, who was an associate of Humphreys, again shortly.

As the No.1 Area Inspectorate investigation under Deputy Assistant Commissioner Sheppard into Drury and Humphreys deepened, and the media continued to follow the story, an official decision was made.

★ ★ ★

New Scotland Yard, South West London, 16 March 1972, late evening

> Commander Kenneth Drury, the officer named in an investigation ordered by the Commissioner a week ago, has been suspended. This Inquiry, which is being conducted by a Deputy Assistant Commissioner of the Metropolitan Police, continues.

It was a short statement, but shocked Drury out of his arrogant audacity. Drury was personally told of his suspension by Deputy Assistant Commissioner Richard Chitty, who himself had been interviewed by DAC Sheppard on 2 March. Chitty was quizzed regarding Drury's application for leave 14–30 January, two weeks of which he had spent on holiday with his wife and Jimmy and Rusty Humphreys, of course. Chitty had phoned Drury at 9 p.m. and told him to report to New Scotland Yard, where he was informed. The newspapers immediately rushed to get Drury's response, and he was incredibly verbose. This was not in line with police procedure when suspended, which was to remain silent, but was perhaps a consequence of Drury's massive ego. The

Evening News ran the headline 'Suspended Yard Chief: I Am Amazed'.

Door-stepped by the London *Evening Standard* early on 7 March at his home in Sidcup, Kent, Drury, wearing cream pyjamas, spoke to reporter John Stevens. Drury:

> I'm shocked. I'm amazed that my suspension happened before I've been seen by the officers investigating the matter. As far as I am concerned, the inquiry is nowhere near complete so I can make really little comment. All I can add is that my wife is absolutely disgusted at this decision. Naturally, I'm very upset over the matter, but I've got nothing to fear from any inquiry. I feel it would clear me of any allegations of improper conduct … I have no idea how long I am suspended for, but I have plenty of other things to do.

The next day Drury was quoted in the *Daily Express* as saying:

> I am a copper and I am paid to do a job and I want to get on with that job. Meanwhile, I will do a few odd jobs around the house until such time as I am vindicated. But you don't catch criminals sitting around in Sidcup.

There was a photograph of Drury walking with his wife Joan and one of their daughters. It was also confirmed that Drury had issued a writ for libel against the *Sunday People*. Just as with Humphreys, the writ would never be followed up, as everything in Manifold's article had been true. Drury repeated that he was innocent in a *Daily Mirror* piece on the same day, and recounted how he had felt when DAC Chitty had told him he was suspended: 'When he told me it really hit me. It took a while to sink in. I knew there had to be an inquiry, but suspension … I felt absolutely sick when I was told.' Not as sick as the truly innocent Murphy, Cooper and McMahon were feeling. On that day they were ten days short of having served the first two years of their life sentences for the Luton Post Office Murder.

Drury's wife Joan said that she was 'disgusted' by her husband's suspension: 'We had a good holiday and everything was completely innocent. If he had done something wrong I would understand, but he hasn't.'

Not only was Drury busy speaking to the newspapers in the days after his suspension, but he was also giving interviews to both radio and television. He appeared on *PM Reports* on the radio on 7 March and on television on ITN *News at Ten* on the same day. For the latter, Drury was interviewed outside his house, and on both programmes he asserted his innocence and said that he was sure that he would be cleared.

But it was three lengthier interviews he gave on 9 March which are really interesting. They came in response to a *Daily Mirror* article that day stating that members of the Flying Squad were protesting, as they did not know if they could mix with criminals any more, and whether they could cultivate informants without facing disciplinary action. As Drury would use the fact that Humphreys was a police informant to explain why he had become so close to him, Drury's thoughts on the matter are illuminating as to his way of thinking, and how he was mounting his defence publicly.

When asked about the disquiet within the Flying Squad on the BBC *World at One* radio programme, Drury said the following:

> I know nothing of this alleged protest at all although I have read on page 2 of today's *Daily Mirror* that my officers are demanding a firm ruling on whether or not they will be allowed to mix with criminals in order that they can carry out their duties. The officers of the Squad are the finest thief-takers in the world, are dedicated in their work and carry out their hazardous and sometimes almost impossible duties in the highest tradition of the Metropolitan Police Service. In order to do this it's absolutely essential that they maintain permanent contact with the criminal because all their efforts are solely reliant on the work of informants. I think the inquiry now en vogue respecting my activities may be separated from this alleged protest ...
>
> However I can appreciate the dilemma in which my officers now find themselves regarding their necessary association with the criminal fraternity. They must now feel that they have got to look over both shoulders before they can do the worthwhile job the public pay them to do. I am firmly of the opinion that any alleged protest by them is not personal and has not been made on my behalf. I am very proud to be

the Commander of such a fine body of men and I feel they only want to know where they are going and not lay themselves open to criticism for doing their duty.

The same feelings were expressed in interviews on the *BBC Evening News* with the prominent broadcaster Richard Baker, and with Michael Blaikie on *BBC2 News*. In the latter broadcast, Drury made the following colourful point about fraternising with criminals:

It's no good going to the vicar's tea party and trying to get any information about organised teams of robbers … People who are prepared to come and help you for the want of the best word, [are] perhaps 'professional informers', and these informants are trusted by their own side.

Drury also stated that the rules about association with criminals were laid down by the Assistant Commissioner (Crime), but that 'the problem seems to be about the definition of association.'

On the following day, the suspended Drury would finally be called into New Scotland Yard to make his statement.

★ ★ ★

Metropolitan Police
No. 1 Area Inspectorate
10th March 1972
Statement of: Kenneth Ronald Drury
Occupation: Commander, C.I.D.
Address: Flying Squad Office, New Scotland Yard, SW1
Statement commenced at 11.40am; Lunch Break at 1.15pm;
Recommenced statement at 2.05pm; Concluded at 4.55pm; Read by Commander Drury and corrected by him in places, which concluded at 6.03pm.
Statement taken in the presence of: DAC F. Sheppard and Commander R. Huntley.

Drury was finally in front of the officers investigating his undesirable relationship with Jimmy Humphreys, four days after being suspended. As a very experienced senior officer, Drury would not have lied about any facts that could be checked. Logistical details relating to the holiday had to be true. Regarding his motivations and relationships with Humphreys and other Soho figures and whether he had paid Humphreys back, Drury had leeway to make his own version of the truth. But Drury knew that No. 1 Area Inspectorate would check into everything he said and would not have risked being caught out on documented facts.

Drury began his statement by saying that Humphreys had not paid for the holiday to Cyprus and Beirut, and that he would come back to that point later. He then stressed that he had no connection to pornography or the Dirty Squad:

> I would first like to say that at no time in my service have I ever had any dealings with pornography or with duties on the Obscene Publications Office, Central Office. I know of no person in the pornographic world of the West End; neither do I know of the location of any of the shops. I have no knowledge whatever of Humphreys being engaged in pornography.

The only truth in that excerpt was that Drury had never served on the Obscene Publications Squad. Of course he knew that Humphreys was a porn merchant, and it is very unlikely that he did not know the locations of Humphreys' operations in Soho. Next, Drury dealt with the fact that he had become friendly with Humphreys, a man with a criminal record: 'I accept that Humphreys is a man with a criminal past, but he was last convicted fourteen years ago and last released from prison ten years ago.' This was true, but it was a barefaced lie when he said of Humphreys, 'So far as I am concerned, he has apparently made every effort to rehabilitate himself, and has apparently done so.'

Drury stipulated that he knew nothing of Humphreys' business interests, and admitted taking his file out while in 'L' Division back in 1951. This was an everyday police procedure and a fact he knew would have been discovered anyway. On when he had first met Humphreys, Drury said, 'In either January or February, 1971, I met Humphreys in a restaurant in the West End, the name of which eludes me for the moment, but this meeting was not by design.'This would have been the party celebrating the promotion of another Flying Squad officer, whose name cannot be verified. This was soon after Drury became Head of the Flying Squad on 1 January, 1971.

On how that first meeting with Humphreys went, Drury expanded:

I was introduced to him, but did not recognise him at that stage, but during the course of conversation, he obviously knew me and I realised who he was. A general conversation ensued and it was patently obvious to me that he knew his way around the West End, and I gave consideration to the possible potential of using him as an informant, but nothing of course was discussed with him regarding this aspect, and he left, asking to see me again.'

Drury said that he had made enquiries about Humphreys, and that his second-in-command in the Flying Squad, Det. Chief Supt Tommy Morrison, had informed him that he believed Humphreys had been a Flying Squad informant in the past. As we learnt earlier, Humphreys had been an informant especially for Tommy Butler during the hunt for the Great Train Robbers in the mid–late 1960s. Drury then gave his explanation for fraternising with Humphreys, especially as Soho was not the Flying Squad's natural territory. It was the Dirty Squad's turf of course, and as we have seen, its Head, Det. Chief Supt Moody, had made a very lucrative network of corruption for himself in Soho. Drury:

I could find no reason which would prohibit me from maintaining a contact with Humphreys, as it is well known that a number of highly organised thieves frequent clubs and like places in the West End, more so when they have successfully committed a crime and are able to spend money accrued from it. In my view, Humphreys' potential as an informer must be good … Since then I have maintained contact with Humphreys and he trusts me implicitly; and I, in return, have considerable trust in him. We meet on varying occasions and he tells me anything he considers will be of interest to me and conversely will find out, if possible, anything I want to know.

Drury then began to go into details about times when Humphreys had helped him as a police informant.

Drury said that Humphreys had supplied him with information about a 'team of south London thieves, one of whom I believe was [redacted], who were actively engaged in committing crimes of Robbery with Violence'. Humphreys had told him that these three men often went to the Astor Club. This was coincidentally where the Kray twins had spent their last night of freedom, before being arrested with hangovers by Leonard 'Nipper' Read on the early morning of 8 May 1968. Humphreys had offered to go to the Astor with him to identify the men, according to Drury. But as Drury was well-known in south London, having served there on 'L' Division for years earlier in his career, Humphreys had reluctantly gone to the Astor with Det. Sgt Legge of the Flying Squad. The gang were put under surveillance and were seen to be active. However, before the Flying Squad could pounce, they were arrested for robbery with violence in west London by No.9 Regional Crime Squad. But as Drury commented in his statement, Humphreys' information had been '100 per cent correct'.

Drury also stated that other information that Humphreys had given to the Flying Squad had led to the arrest 'of a team of violent thieves who committed an armed robbery which is known as "the Bond Street job".' Humphreys had also 'imparted information to Det. Inspector Miller of the Flying Squad, and I believe this officer has been successful as a result of it'. Added to this, Humphreys had told Drury about 'a team of English thieves who were wanted for an offence of attempted murder, I believe, in Sweden', and that Humphreys had 'located some of them in Switzerland and also told me when one was due to return to this country'. Det. Inspector Miller had also worked on this case, along with Det. Inspector Bland. Bland has previously been mentioned in the Flying Squad operation to find the kidnappers and killers of Muriel McKay in early 1970, and will feature again later. Bland had arrested one of the men at London Airport, but neither Sweden nor Switzerland had pursued his extradition.

Earlier, we learnt of the information that Drury said Humphreys supplied regarding the murder of Det. Constable Coward in Reading in

June 1971 by Arthur Skingle and Peter Sparrow, both of whom had been convicted. Drury had travelled to Reading on the day after the murder with a detective chief inspector (name redacted) to assist. Drury said that he had thought that Skingle would return to the West End, where he often could be found, as he took drugs:

> Drury: I telephoned Humphreys and made an appointment to see him in the West End at 8.30 p.m. … I spoke to Humphreys [with the Det. Chief Inspector also present] in an endeavour to ascertain where Skingle might frequent.'

Humphreys had given the names of four clubs, where they went, and found that Skingle had recently been there to score drugs. But they just missed him. The next day, Skingle was arrested in a hotel in Holborn, central London by members of the Flying Squad. Drury can be believed on this, as the source of information could be checked quickly and independently with other members of the Flying Squad before Drury could coach those supportive of him. So, as has long been thought in the underworld, the criminally very well-connected Humphreys acted as a serial police informant. This was something which Humphreys would of course have wanted to keep very quiet. Therefore, not only was Humphreys paying enormous sums to police officers, he was aiding the apprehension of fellow criminals to lubricate the free running of his own vice activities.

Drury then set up the reason for going on holiday with Humphreys, by linking the fact about Humphreys acting as an informant. Drury could then introduce the dubious theory that he and his wife had gone to Cyprus and Beirut with Jimmy and Rusty Humphreys to search for the fugitive Great Train Robber Ronnie Biggs. Although in a statement to the No. 1 Area Inspectorate on 6 March 1972, the day of Drury's suspension, Det. Chief Supt Morrison, Drury's No.2 in the Flying Squad, backed up the Biggs story:

> Morrison: Sometime in December, 1971, he [Drury] told me in the strictest confidence that he had certain information that Biggs was possibly

in Cyprus … Mr Drury did not disclose the source of his information and neither did I ask. He told me that only Chief Inspector [redacted], and myself, would know the main reason for his holiday.

In fact, Drury had sent a postcard from Cyprus. It had been pinned on the Flying Squad noticeboard for weeks, the short message reading 'Wish you were all here', creating much gossip. So much for Drury's careful discretion …

Drury said that in mid-November 1971 he had received information that Biggs was in Cyprus from a source in south London, his old patch. Also, that earlier, in the middle of 1971, he had learnt that Biggs was in Malta, and associating with a man named Flowers. Two people, including then Det. Sgt Blakeney (by March 1972 a Det. Inspector) of 'C' Division at Bow Street had gone to Malta to look for Biggs, posing as tourists, the trip financed by the Police Fund. In fact, Blakeney would be dismissed from the Met later in the 1970s, along with a detective sergeant. Drury said that as Head of the Flying Squad, he had liaised with the Assistant Commissioner (Crime) (ACC) on this, and that the ACC had suggested that the officers travelled on false passports, but that Drury had disagreed, and in the end they had travelled on their own passports. However, the Malta trip had been leaked to the press, and the Maltese police had been annoyed as they had not been informed. Drury said that the Maltese police had not been told as they could not be trusted.

Drury added that in late November 1971, he had sought the advice of Det. Chief Inspector Wilson of the Flying Squad about whether Biggs could be in Cyprus. Wilson had previously been in the British Police Unit in Cyprus and still had Cypriot informants in Britain. Wilson had asked around, according to Drury, and while he could not confirm that Biggs was in Cyprus, he 'gave every indication he may well have been there'. Drury then explained that he knew that Humphreys had 'a number of Cypriot contacts in the West End' and so asked Humphreys to make enquiries too. Humphreys did this and came back to Drury saying that the information about Biggs being in Cyprus 'bore some truth'.

Drury continued his statement by saying that he had arranged to take his wife, who had been ill recently, on holiday to Spain in February or

March 1972 with Det. Chief Inspector Smith. But when he found out the information about Biggs, he had decided to go to Cyprus instead, to have a holiday and look for Biggs at the same time. Drury said that he had 'discussed the matter in full with my Chief Inspectors'. In fact, Drury's deputy, Det. Chief Supt Morrison, had said that he knew about the switch from Spain to Cyprus in the statement he had given four days earlier. Manifold had told Humphreys of his intention of publishing his exposure of the holiday on 25 February and Humphreys undoubtedly would have immediately warned Drury. But had Drury spoken to Morrison between 25 February and 6 March when the latter made his statement, informing him about the Biggs angle, or had he told Morrison before the holiday had taken place? Due to what would come out later, the former is far more likely.

Drury said he had then asked his wife if she would be willing to go to Cyprus instead, and she had agreed. Also that Det. Chief Inspector Smith hadn't minded the change of plan about not going to Spain. So how did Drury explain exactly how he and his wife Joan ended up going on holiday with Jimmy and Rusty Humphreys?

> Drury: In consequence of the decision I had made, I mentioned it to Humphreys, asking if he would endeavour to obtain some further information for me. He then told me that he had received further information to the effect that Biggs was believed to be in Cyprus and had been given to understand that he had been seen in clubs there. He then stated that he too was thinking of taking a holiday and, providing I had no objection, he would like to accompany me to Cyprus with our wives and as he knew Biggs personally and had contacts on the island, through his association with Cypriots in London, he may well be able to be useful out there. I could see nothing wrong in this because I do not accept that a man of Humphreys' calibre, who has obviously rehabilitated himself, having kept clear of crime for over nine years, should be viewed with any undue suspicion or have his past raked up.

Humphreys had given Drury thousands of pounds in bribes by this point, plus many gifts and much hospitality. Drury also knew full well that Humphreys had not rehabilitated himself of course. Humphreys had not been prosecuted for any serious offence for over nine years, but the main reason for this was the huge sums of money he was paying to Drury, Moody, Virgo and other officers for 'protection' and turning a blind eye. Drury had of course also smoothed out a feud between Humphreys, one of the biggest pornographers in Soho and probably the country, and Bernie Silver, a ponce, pimp and pornographer, one of the most powerful men in Soho's underworld. As always, Drury's audacity was astounding.

Drury then spoke about a Bill then currently being considered in Parliament, which would mean that any offences committed more than six years before that date would not be taken into consideration. Drury's reasoning was that as Humphreys had not been convicted of anything (aside from several minor club licensing convictions, for which fines were paid) for more than nine years, he was not a criminal in the eyes of the law any more. This indicates how rehearsed was Drury's statement. Since Manifold had told Humphreys about the article exposing the holiday, almost two weeks had passed. That was a great deal of time for Drury to plan his explanation, and one wonders why No. 1 Area Inspectorate didn't interview Drury first, rather than last. Surely Drury should have been called in to New Scotland Yard on 27 February, the day the *Sunday People* piece appeared if necessary, or as soon as possible. The reason for this may have been sensitivities due to Drury being a very senior officer and Head of the Flying Squad, so other inquiries had to be made first.

Next, Drury reinforced his reason for going to look for Biggs in Cyprus. Drury pointed out that the late Tommy Butler, the former Head of the Flying Squad, had used his leave on 'three or four occasions' to look for Bruce Reynolds in the South of France. Drury had tried to bribe Reynolds in the late 1940s, it should be remembered. Then Drury went into the logistics of the booking of the holiday, saying that it had been agreed that Humphreys would book it at Thomas Cook. This was because Humphreys had a branch near his office (true) and because Humphreys had to book dates which fitted with his business arrangements (probably true), whereas Drury could take leave at almost any time (true). But Humphreys had also paid for the holiday and Drury knew that he had to convince his investigators that he had paid Humphreys back for his half-share. If Humphreys had paid for the holiday, and it could be proved that Drury had not paid him back, then the heat really would be on Drury.

> Drury: I met Humphreys and on this occasion he told me he had booked the tickets for a holiday in Cyprus and that we were to stay in the Grecian Hotel in Famagusta. The holiday was booked from 14th to 28th January, 1972. I then discussed payment with him, the cost of the holiday on the part of my wife and myself, and he told me £250. I would like it borne in mind that I had no control of the booking, neither did I see any documents relating to it. I at first considered paying Humphreys by cheque but changed my mind and, in due course, paid him in cash. I suppose, to avoid any misunderstanding, that I should mention that the cash used to pay Humphreys was drawn from a Savings Club which I drew out in December, 1971, where I was paid the sum of £157.12, and £50 which was drawn on a cheque through my bank and the remainder from savings of my wife and myself.

It was proven by No. 1 Area Inspectorate that Drury had drawn out £157.12 from the Flying Squad Savings Club in December, 1971. Officers of the Squad would save an amount weekly and then have a cash sum for Christmas. In fact, there was no proof that Drury had paid Humphreys back, and DAC Sheppard's final report on this initial investigation of Drury's association with Humphreys would state that Drury 'cannot give a precise date or produce documentary evidence of paying Humphreys'. Did that £157.12 really go to Humphreys, and the £50 cheque and savings held by Drury and his wife? Or did Humphreys pay for everything, with Drury accepting a freebie, this being the real reason for going on holiday with Humphreys? In his statements, Humphreys had said that Drury had paid him back, in January, not in December as Drury said. But as we shall see, Humphreys would completely change his story two-and-a-half months later in late May 1972.

Drury said that he had booked in at the Grecian Hotel in Famagusta, Cyprus, with his wife and Jimmy and Rusty Humphreys, using his own name and occupation 'Commander Metro Police'. This was confirmed by police enquiries. No. 1 Area Inspectorate had been very thorough, the Grecian Hotel had been investigated, and it was described as being 'white-painted, concrete and glass' and had been built just seven years previously. It had seventy-five rooms, each with a balcony overlooking the sea, with tennis courts, a heated swimming pool, sauna, roof garden and a card-room. It also had an underground tavern with a 'nightclub atmosphere' where traditional music was played accompanied by a 'glass dance' where a dancer moved across the dance floor with seven glasses on his head. Photographs would later emerge of the holiday, the first taken by Jimmy Humphreys, showing a smiling Drury and his wife on the outward flight to Cyprus. Another was of the two couples sitting opposite each other having dinner in Cyprus, taken by somebody else.

Regarding who paid for the day-to-day incidental costs of the holiday, Drury was of course at pains to stress that he had paid his share. He said that Humphreys had paid for the hiring of a Vauxhall Viva hire car (easily checked), but that he had paid for the petrol to run it (not checkable). Drury stated that 'the rest of the expenditure incurred on the holiday was equitably shared by both of us', and this included meals and drinks. On the trip to Beirut in Lebanon, which Drury said they had decided to take after Humphreys had made enquiries with his contacts in London:

> Humphreys was in constant contact with people in London, whose identity I do not know, and he suggested we should go to Beirut for a weekend to see the Casino and he also wished to visit a club called the Crazey Horse, because he was of the opinion he may be able to find out something about Biggs … we visited the Crazey Horse … and the Casino, but nothing was found regarding Biggs by Mr Humphreys, or for that matter, in turn, myself.

Again, Drury said that all costs for the Beirut trip had been equally shared by himself and Humphreys. Drury went into detail about who paid for what sundry items and then paid the other back.

On the return to Cyprus, Humphreys had arranged, through his 'associates', for Drury to meet the second-in-command of the Turkish police in Famagusta Old City. The island was of course segregated by Greek and Turkish regions, and they had separate police forces. The Turkish policeman that Drury met had apparently attended a detective course in Wakefield in Yorkshire. But Drury conveniently told No. 1 Area Inspectorate, 'I was far from impressed with him as a police officer. In consequence, I considered it prudent to mention nothing of Biggs.' They also visited the Savoy and Venus nightclubs, Nicosia racecourse, all 'coupled with the incidental chance of finding Biggs, but we did not do so'.

Through Humphreys' contacts, Drury also met an ex-Cypriot policeman called Mehmet Aziz, who was now a barrister practising in the Turkish quarter of Nicosia.

> Drury: I learned he is the brother of, I believe, the owner of the Celebrity Club in the West End of London [in London, this man was known as John Mehmet], who I have spoken to I suppose on two or three occasions. I also understood that he was related or was a friend of another club owner, whose name was only mentioned as Selim, but who, at that stage, I had never met; nor did I know him.

Five days before Drury made his statement, on Sunday 5 March, Laurie Manifold had published another article in the *Sunday People*, a week after the Drury–Humphreys exposure. This time the front-page headline was 'Another Indiscreet Holiday' and the focus was the Fraud Squad. The allegation was made that Det. Chief Supt Kenneth Etheridge, No. 2 in the Fraud Squad, had stayed at Selim Mehmet's flat in Cyprus. It was the same Selim.

As well as dining at the barrister's house, Drury and Humphreys went on to meet and have dinner with the barrister and Selim Mehmet, and they spent a day in Kyrenia with the latter. It might be remembered that Selim Mehmet had sold Jimmy Humphreys a premises at 58 Greek Street in 1970. In 1972, Selim Mehmet was the proprietor of the Boulogne Restaurant at 27 Gerrard Street, Soho, which had been established fifty years earlier in 1922. According to Manifold in the *Sunday People* of 5 March 1972, at the Boulogne 'hostesses offer their vice services to customers', with such arrangements being made through a waiter, and the price was around £30 for sex. An advertisement for the Boulogne Restaurant at the time stated, 'You'll never be lonely at the Boulogne'.

Selim Mehmet had in fact already been interviewed by No. 1 Area Inspectorate and given a statement several days before Drury. Selim Mehmet was 34 years old, and he said in his statement, 'I've known Humphreys round the West End for several years ... I did not know Commander Drury until I met him in Nicosia in January 1972.' Humphreys had asked him to supply the addresses of his friends in Cyprus, and he had given Humphreys the address of his solicitor, Mehmet Aziz, but did not say that he was related to him. At the dinner in a fish restaurant, Selim Mehmet said that all the men had wanted to pay, but Mehmet Aziz had insisted, as he knew the restaurant owner.

When they had tea on another day, Drury had paid the bill, he said. Selim Mehmet also mentioned Biggs:

> During the meal there was a conversation between Mr Humphreys and myself. He asked me what I think about Biggs being in Cyprus. I understood he was saying that Biggs might be in Cyprus and that he was asking my opinion as to such a possibility. I expressed the view that Biggs might be in Cyprus as I think Cyprus is freer than Australia [another place where Biggs was thought to be] ... While we were talking like this Mr Drury overheard our discussion and told off Mr Humphreys for talking to me. He indicated in the manner in which he spoke that he did not want Humphreys to talk on that subject.

Selim Mehmet said that he had not seen Drury since the holiday, but that he had seen Humphreys on 1 February 1972. He had read the *Sunday People* article on 28 February, and the following day reporters from three different newspapers had gone to his office at the Boulogne in Gerrard Street. Selim Mehmet also confirmed that he had a flat in Cyprus, in Kyrenia, presumably the one in which Det. Chief Supt Etheridge of the Fraud Squad was alleged to have stayed.

In his statement, Drury said that when he arrived at the barrister Mehmet Aziz's house in Cyprus, there were two other men there:

one of whom I recognised as the owner of the Hirondelle Club, who I only know as Jack, and the other was a man who was introduced to me as Selim, the owner of the Boulogne Club, or restaurant, in the West End. I had never seen this man before; knew nothing of him, nor of his business interests, and I had no reason to believe he was any other than the polite businessman he was introduced as; nor had I any knowledge of the fact that he has a criminal record …

Selim Mehmet's criminal record sheet is in the Met files, and shows that in September 1960 he had received a fifteen-month sentence for 'uttering forged documents (forged banknotes)'. In September 1964 he had been fined for four charges of 'being a keeper of a place selling refreshments which did permit disorderly conduct, did suffer prostitutes to remain in a refreshment house' and 'permitting public dancing on premises not licensed for such a purpose'. In March 1965 he had been fined £5 for assaulting a police officer, and received another £5 fine for 'being present for the purpose of effecting a betting transaction'. In February 1968 he had been fined £10 for taking part in unlawful gaming.

Drury then wanted to clear up a rumour going round:

I have heard rumblings through various sources of my information that I am supposed to have gone on holiday with Humphreys and his wife before one of these occasions alleging that I went to Greece with him. This is quite untrue. In fact, since leaving the army in 1946, I have never been abroad with anyone at all.

He stated that both he and his wife had only had their passports issued in December 1971 or January 1972, specifically for the Cyprus holiday with Humphreys and his wife. Following that, Drury made his allegation that a journalist delving into the Luton Post Office Murder convictions had a grudge against him, as detailed at the end of Chapter Two – an obvious ploy to get his word in first in case that journalist uncovered hard evidence of Drury's complex and wilfully venal actions in that tragic case.

The next move for Drury in his statement was to say that he had issued a writ against the *Sunday People* through his solicitor, A. Kramer & Co. He explained that while the main front page story about his holiday with Humphreys had not directly alleged corruption, when read in conjunction with the separate article on pages three and four of that day's paper, that would be the overall impression. Drury then made his closing statement in defence of himself:

> I have never, during the course of my service, ever been accused of or been the subject of enquiry into any allegation of corruption or like matters. The '*Sunday People*' article, according to them, make it quite plain that they are not alleging any impropriety on my part but the innuendo is that I have accepted a favour from Humphreys, that he paid for my holiday in Cyprus and the Lebanon and that I have been improperly associating with a convicted thief. I do not consider that my association with Humphreys has been in any way improper, for the reasons I have set out in this statement. I have at no stage ever asked favours of Humphreys, other than asking him to supply information, but certainly not a favour which would affect me personally as a police officer. In turn, Humphreys at no stage has ever asked me for any favour or consideration to be given to him in any capacity as a police officer.

The dishonesty and arrogance of Drury here is truly mind-blowing. He had accepted thousands of pounds from Humphreys, plus gifts and hospitality, and as we will see, Humphreys would soon claim that he had paid for the holiday in full. Drury had also done Humphreys a 'favour', for a large price, almost a quarter of his annual salary – he had sorted out the dispute between Humphreys and Bernie Silver for more than £1000.

DAC Sheppard and Commander Huntley then asked Drury some questions, chiefly details about the paying back of Humphreys for the holiday. Most interestingly, Drury said that he had never met Humphreys on the latter's business premises, and had specifically never gone to the hub of Humphreys' Soho empire, the Queen's Club on Berwick Street. This is strangely probably true, as Drury had no need to visit Humphreys at work. They had been meeting in exclusive restaurants and hotels, as well as the Hogarth Club in Soho, the latter not run by Humphreys. Incidentally, the Met files show that Humphreys had been busy covering his tracks regarding his links to pornography. On 6 March, within days of giving his statements, he transferred the telephone line registration from 'R.A. Hustler' into the name of another person, the new name redacted in the document.

Drury had been given a Form 163 by No.1 Area Inspectorate, and there is a copy of this in the Met files. It lays out the misconduct that Drury is accused of, and of course centres on the holiday with Humphreys, a convicted criminal, and the latter's attendance at the annual Flying Squad dinner. It also mentions Selim Mehmet and his criminal record too. There is no accusation against Drury of taking illegal and improper payments from Humphreys, and it only mentions Humphreys' vice activities as quoted from the *Sunday People*. Thanks to the statements of members of the Dirty Squad, Humphreys was not 'officially' a pornographer in the eyes of the Metropolitan Police. But it would all come out in time. The last misconduct charge against Drury on a second Form 163 was that he had contravened Metropolitan Police rules by giving media interviews and 'unauthorised statements' between 27 February and 10 March 1972.

A 14 March statement given by Commander Robert Huntley of No.1 Area Inspectorate, one of the officers present when Drury gave his statement on 10 March, shows that the worm was beginning to wriggle. It concerns the moment at the end of the day when DAC Sheppard gave Drury his second Form 163 regarding his unauthorised media interviews. The first Form 163 had been given to Drury at 11.36 a.m.:

Commander Huntley: At 6.05pm DAC Sheppard said 'There was one matter I did not include on form 163 served on you earlier. I therefore have to serve you with an additional form. Once again I draw your attention to the caution at the bottom of the form.' Mr Sheppard read the caution again and then served Mr Drury with form 163. Commander Drury said 'I have nothing to say in respect of this.' Mr Sheppard said 'Mr Drury I must remind you that General Orders must be complied with in this respect.' Mr Drury did not answer and he left the office.'

The final report on No. 1 Area Inspectorate's investigation was submitted to the Deputy Commissioner, Robert Mark, by DAC Sheppard on 16 March 1972. It was detailed and had ninety-six points, recommending disciplinary action against Drury for the following offences: acting in a manner reasonably likely to bring discredit on the reputation of the Force by improperly associating with James William Humphreys; without good and sufficient cause taking part in the radio programme *World at One*, the *BBC News* and *BBC2 News*. A further eleven minor charges were thought to be able to be 'met by some firm advice'. There was no evidence to support the charge that Drury had 'improperly accepted a gratuity' from Humphreys and for improperly associating with Selim Mehmet.

★ ★ ★

In order to fully understand the suspended Commander Drury's next move, we have to understand the massive upheavals that had been taking place at the top of the Metropolitan Police. Largely due to the newspapers, there had been open rumours of Met officers taking bribes and 'verballing' or intimidating suspects, and sharing in the proceeds of crime for some time. The corruption at West End Central in the early 1960s and 'Tanky' Challenor, the *Times* Inquiry, and numerous newspaper articles had added to this gossip. This hadn't escaped the attention of the Home Office, which of course is the governmental department that oversees policing in Britain.

Of course the speculation was true, and then some. In early 1967, the Home Secretary Roy Jenkins summoned Robert Mark (who would be knighted in 1973) to his office in the House of Commons, which was situated just behind the Speaker of the House's chair. Mark had served in the Manchester City Police from 1937, alongside Frank Williamson, who was obstructed in the *Times* Inquiry. Mark had worked his way up to become the Chief Constable of Leicester in 1957. Mark was a man of forthright opinions, determination, and above all, integrity. Roy Jenkins had met Mark before, as Mark was on Lord Mountbatten's Standing Advisory Committee into the Penal System. Mark had in fact just been involved in looking into the escape of Frank 'Mad Axeman' Mitchell, a physically huge man who was unstable, from Dartmoor Prison in December 1966. Mitchell had been helped in fleeing and harboured by the Krays, but who soon ordered Mitchell's murder when he became restless and difficult to handle.

Jenkins offered Mark the post of Assistant Commissioner in the Metropolitan Police, and Mark accepted, taking it up in March 1967. The Metropolitan Police then had approximately 22,000 officers. Mark's role was largely administrative, in 'D' Department. Sir Joseph Simpson was then Commissioner of the Metropolitan Police with John Waldron as his Deputy Commissioner, until Simpson died in office in March 1968. Mark had had a strained relationship with Simpson, although in his memoirs Mark spoke highly of him. Eight days after Simpson died the new Home Secretary Jim Callaghan called Mark in and told him that he was being considered for the post of Commissioner. Callaghan wanted Mark's thoughts on this. In his memoirs, Mark said, 'I told him that I thought I was no less well qualified professionally than any other candidate, and perhaps better than most, but that to appoint me would be mistaken, if not disastrous.'

Mark explained to Callaghan that his appointment as Commissioner would be 'bitterly resented by the very people I would need to make a success of the job and that I had no doubt that some of them would lend all their endeavours to ensure the opposite'. Mark had been in the Met for just a year, and was obviously seen as and felt like an outsider within it. The internal politics within the CID hierarchy which Mark would have to face when he eventually did become Commissioner and began to clean up the force would prove Mark's point. In 1978, when he had retired, Mark felt that his decision not to go forward as a candidate for Commissioner in 1968 was 'the wisest decision I ever made'.

Callaghan asked Mark who he felt should be the Commissioner. Mark said that the Deputy Commissioner John Waldron should take the job, and that when Waldron had reached the age of 60 in two years, a successor could be appointed who had been thoroughly evaluated. When Mark was called back on 5 April 1968, Callaghan told him that he was going to do what Mark proposed. Waldron was to be the new Met

Commissioner, and that Mark himself was to be Deputy Commissioner. This did not mean that he would automatically become Commissioner when Waldron retired, said Callaghan, but, 'you will have the chance to see what you can do.' So Mark was in place to learn the job and get used to the Metropolitan Police.

But Mark soon realised that being Deputy Commissioner wasn't a fulfilling post, in fact, even Waldron, who had just left the position, told him early on that it was 'the worst job in the force'. Like many deputies, Mark had no real power, as that all lay with the Commissioner and individual Deputy Assistant Commissioners, especially the DAC (Crime). Peter Brodie was the DAC (Crime), the man who would soon discount Frank Williamson's concerns about the corruption of Det. Chief Supt Moody on the *Times* Inquiry. This happened in November 1969 when Mark had been Deputy Commissioner for just over eighteen months. It was the *Times* Inquiry that triggered Mark to deal with the corruption within the CID, and the closed shop mentality he found around him. But he would not have the power until he was Commissioner, although he knew that the government were now behind change in the Met and the rooting out of bent officers:

> From that point on, I never felt alone. Rightly or wrongly, I was con-
> vinced that the Home Office had at last realised that all was not well and
> I was in the happy position of knowing that any kind of enquiry could
> only redound to my advantage and the exposure of a situation which had
> already lasted far too long.

Mark recounted that Peter Brodie had thought that he would be the next Commissioner, as did many in the CID. It is obvious that there was some animosity between Mark and Brodie. The latter represented the old guard, the one that Mark wanted to reorganise and to which he devoted a chapter in his memoirs entitled 'The Battle for the Control of the CID'. Mark had proposed the creation of an anti-corruption unit at New Scotland Yard, called A10, which would handle all serious complaints against the Metropolitan Police. Brodie managed to persuade Commissioner Waldron not to adopt this. But Mark's time would come.

In fact, John Waldron would remain Commissioner until 16 April 1972, having been granted an extension by Ted Heath's Conservative Government. For some time it had become obvious that Mark would be the next Commissioner, and not Brodie. In mid March 1972, Brodie went to hospital suffering from 'excessive strain'. He never went back to the Metropolitan Police. That strain had no doubt been partly caused by the fight that Brodie and others in the CID had with Deputy Commissioner Mark over Drury, and the shifting of the direction of power it signposted.

In the same month, it was Mark who pushed Commissioner Waldron to suspend Drury, Head of the Flying Squad, after his links to Humphreys were exposed. In his memoirs, Mark recalled the fight with the CID he'd had to get Drury suspended:

> This inevitably led to a real showdown. The CID argument was that suspension would undermine CID morale, encourage criminals, and do irreparable damage to the reputation of the force … My reply was that failure to suspend would confirm the public's worst suspicions … It resulted in a final trial of strength between 'C' Department and me, with the unfortunate Commissioner in the middle.

That was the real reason that Drury was so shocked at his suspension. Before Mark came along as Deputy Commissioner and had limited clout, and then real power as Commissioner, Drury would have been allowed to continue as Head of the Flying Squad. And when the media furore had died down, he probably would have got an internal rap on the knuckles. But times were changing.

Mark became Commissioner on 17 April 1972, and A10, his anti-corruption unit, was put into immediate operation. During the first few months that Mark was Commissioner, suspension of officers averaged around fifty a month, a massive increase, and this was the work of A10. When he made his Inaugural Address, Mark spoke the line which would echo throughout the CID, the Metropolitan Police as a whole, and the British public. It undoubtedly induced fear in bent officers, forcing some to clean up fast, but for others the corruption they had been involved in was so great that it was too late. Commissioner Mark said: 'A good police force is one that catches more criminals than it employs.'

Drury must have realised that Mark was the surgeon who was going to try to cut the cancer of corruption from the comatose Metropolitan Police. And as we now know, Drury had been guilty of far more serious corruption than the holiday and the initial association with Humphreys indicated. Drury probably knew deep down that he was finished, as soon as he was suspended, but he held on for seven weeks, until 1 May 1972, when he resigned.

The Met issued the following statement: 'Commander Kenneth Drury, who was suspended from duty on 6 March, pending the outcome of an inquiry into an alleged contravention of police discipline, has offered his resignation from the force. This has been accepted with effect from midnight tonight.'

Drury gave more interviews to the newspapers, and on the night of his resignation he spoke to the *Times*, standing outside his home in Sidcup, Kent, wearing a black suit and white shirt and smoking a cigarette.

> My resignation was entirely my own decision. I have had it in mind for some time now. I was not called in today. I resigned on my own volition and the resignation went through normal channels. The Commissioner has accepted my resignation. It was a matter for me and my conscience. Regret is probably the wrong word. I will miss the esprit de corps of the force and of course I will have some regrets about it.

He added that he had not lined up a new job, nor did he have any immediate plans.

It is extremely likely that Drury's friends in the CID had told him that there was no way back. By resigning, he kept his pension, and he had no idea how much more A10 would dig out about the depths of his misdeeds. Pandora's lid was being prised open, and those involved in corruption within the CID were justifiably very worried and upset. The fact that Drury was soon replaced as the Head of the Flying Squad by Det. Chief Supt John Locke, aged 49, who was specially drafted in from outside the Squad, showed that Mark wanted the change to come from the top and work down. Locke, who now became a Commander, had been the favourite to take command of A10, and choosing him showed that Mark was going to steer the elite squads in an honest direction. Mark wanted to show the 150-strong Flying Squad that their thief-taking exploits were greatly valued, but that there was no room for corruption. When the true levels of wrongdoing were exposed, the Flying Squad as Drury knew it would be finished within a few years.

It was a massive turnaround for Drury, who just a few months before had been the favoured candidate to take the high-flying post of National Co-Ordinator of the Regional Crime Squads. This is confirmed by 'Nipper' Read, another candidate, in his autobiography. So if Drury's links hadn't been exposed, he could well have risen higher than Head of the Flying Squad. But what Drury did next showed that he had lost none of his audacity. He was not one to go quietly. Drury's hubris would help lead to not only his own final downfall, but that of many other corrupt officers of both the Flying Squad and Dirty Squad.

5

A BEAUTIFUL FRIENDSHIP ENDS

News of the World, Sunday, 21 May 1972

EX-FLYING SQUAD CHIEF TALKS AT LAST

My Friends In The Underworld
by ex-Commander Kenneth Drury

FUNNY, isn't it? My friends in the underworld made me one of Scotland Yard's top coppers. Now, through keeping in with them, I'm out in the cold. A few weeks ago I was chief of the Flying Squad, one of the plum jobs in the police world. Now I'm out. On the scrap heap.

I'm an ex-copper with a reputation that, in the public's mind, would appear to be a bit tarnished to say the least.

How did it all happen? What went wrong? Now, for the first time, I'm telling the whole story.

Three weeks after he resigned, Drury sold his 'story' to the News of the World, one of the Sunday People's great rivals. He was allegedly paid £10,000. Covering the whole of the front page and page three, it was written as Drury spoke, with necessary expletives deleted. There were also photographs of a miserable-looking Drury. Plus, one of Drury and his wife with June 'Rusty' Humphreys, which Humphreys probably took on the Cyprus holiday; a sinister mug-shot of Humphreys; an old snap of a scantily clad June 'Rusty' Humphreys as stripper 'Rusty Gaynor'; and one of Drury shaking hands with Prince Philip at a charity lunch.

Here's Drury, the innocent victim:

> Everybody's read how the wife and I went to Cyprus for a holiday with Jimmy Humphreys, the Soho 'strip king', and his missus. Years ago he was an out-and-out villain with form up to your elbow. But though he's been going straight for ten years, it appears I shouldn't have done it. When it all came out I was suspended. I'll never forget those first few days after it happened. I've never been so choked in my life. It was like a blow well below the belt.

Choked? Below the belt? Not as choked as Murphy, Cooper and McMahon were, serving life sentences for the Luton Post Office Murder, after being framed by Drury. That's below the belt.

Drury then went on to speak of his love for Scotland Yard, a love he had felt ever since he had first 'stepped out on the beat as a dead green young PC down in south London'. This was shortly before he became a detective constable and propositioned Bruce Reynolds. Following that, he introduced the main thrust of his article, his use of informants. This was of course his defence for associating with Humphreys. 'On the vast majority of cases I've dealt with – and they go from murder downwards – informants have played a vital role.' Indeed they had, as in the case of Alf Mathews, who lied to convict innocent men, at the behest of Drury, both of them sharing in the reward. Then he detailed how he had immediately known where Frederick Sewell was, who had murdered Det. Supt Gerald Richardson in Blackpool. Sewell had been jailed for life in March 1972. Drury recounted how he had got a tip-off about Sewell's whereabouts from an informant 'codenamed Greedy George', and so sent a team of Flying Squad 'heavies' down to Orpington, Kent. But unfortunately, Drury said they had missed Sewell 'by only 20 minutes'. Drury called informants 'the lifeblood of a copper's job':

> Every copper worth his salt has informants. And I'd wager I'm not the only officer to have socialised with one. There are rules governing a police officer's conduct with informants but, honestly, if you followed them literally you could never catch a single thief. If a detective got into bother every time he bought a quick gin for a tart there would be no Scotland Yard.

Drury stated that the most he had ever paid a 'snout' was £400, which had led to the seizure of £1 million of LSD and 'a dockful of nasty villains'. He added that he knew of an informant being paid £700 in a case involving very serious crime. These single payment figures were less than Drury had received in one go from a serious criminal himself, but no mention of that of course.

Drury would go on to heavily insinuate that Jimmy Humphreys was an informant, which can be confirmed now. It's interesting to note that Drury first went into detail about the dangers of being an informant and being exposed as one. 'It's obviously bloody dangerous. They live on a time bomb. Their lives and those of their families aren't worth two pen'orth of cold gin if they are rumbled.' Just a few paragraphs later: 'I've had informants that I wouldn't let within a mile of the missus. But Jimmy Humphreys, to hark back to Cyprus again, has always been a perfect gentleman with me.' Drury might as well have said 'Jimmy Humphreys is a police informer.'

Drury's article ended with 'Next Week – Famous Villains I Have Known'. Humphreys must have been spitting out his cornflakes all over his silk monogrammed pyjamas by the time he finished the article that Sunday morning. He could have been in serious danger, perhaps for his life, if heavy criminals believed Drury and word got around that he was a 'grass'.

A report dated 15 June 1972 by DAC Sheppard of No.1 Area Inspectorate in the Met files shows that Humphreys acted fast. Sheppard wrote that on Friday 26 May, five days after Drury's 'story' was published, Humphreys' solicitor phoned the No.1 Area Inspectorate office, based at Paddington Green Police Station, London W2, and asked to see Sheppard. The report also gives the details of Drury's revelations about informants in the *News of the World*. Sheppard had arranged to meet with Humphreys' solicitor on Tuesday 30 May. But Humphreys made a public move before that meeting could take place. Damage had been caused to the Metropolitan Police's public image by the original *Sunday People* article of 27 February, followed by Drury's suspension and resignation. This would seem minor, however, compared to what Humphreys now revealed:

News of the World, Sunday 28 May 1972

YARD CHIEF SENSATION

Soho's King Jim claims: I lied to protect Drury …
my friendship with him cost me about £5,000

Beneath the article by Alan Whittaker and Peter Earle was a photograph of Jimmy and Rusty Humphreys sitting opposite Kenneth and Joan Drury at London's Talk of the Town. Everybody was smiling except for Jimmy, probably because he knew he was paying for the evening out. Humphreys was quoted beneath the picture: 'We went out together 58 times. I always paid the bills.'

Humphreys said that he had lied to No.1 Area Inspectorate's inquiry to protect Drury, and that he had already retracted his statement. But as we will see, that would not be done until two days later. Humphreys was very forthcoming in the article. Regarding Drury and himself going to Cyprus to find Ronnie Biggs, Humphreys backtracked:

This was absolute rubbish. When Commander Drury learned that his superiors at the Yard were aware of our holiday together, he asked me to tell this story about Biggs ... The week after we returned from Cyprus I saw Ken Drury and we went to the World Sporting Club at the Grosvenor House. He told me some of his colleagues had leaked a story to the Press about our holiday together [it was in fact Joey Pyle]. On the Thursday he telephoned me and I met him and another senior officer. Drury said "If any reporters come and see you, tell them we were in Cyprus looking for Biggs because we'd received an underworld tipoff.' ... I was protecting a friend. And now, for money, this friend publicly calls me a 'grass' and my wife an ex-stripper. I've never grassed or informed on anyone. It's true that my wife used to appear in striptease shows. She was also a dancer. At no time has she ever appeared in the nude in public.

In actual fact, Rusty Humphreys was just about to start a four-month sentence in Holloway Prison for possession of a firearm.

Humphreys also stressed that he had paid for the entire Cyprus and Beirut holiday. He had also attended the 1971 FA Cup Final football match at Wembley stadium with Drury. Incidentally, this took place on 8 May, and Arsenal beat Liverpool 2–1. But the most ominous disclosure made by Humphreys that day was that he kept diaries, which contained details of all of his appointments, who with and where. This would be the information bomb waiting to go off in time.

Beneath Humphreys' exclusive on an inside page, under the headline 'Nothing But Aggro, Says Drury', Drury's reply to Humphreys' claims was given. He had been interviewed the previous evening. Drury said that he had always 'paid his way' when with Mr and Mrs Humphreys:

Drury: I don't care what Humphreys is saying. He's talking rubbish. The truth should be well known by now. I've never varied my story by a single word ... His allegation that our friendship in one year has cost him £5,000, well, I just wouldn't know ... I admit that I went to all sorts of social functions and events with him, but he knew the West End better than anybody, and I regarded it as part of my job as a copper to keep myself informed. To me he was just a successful West End businessman.

All I knew was that he owned various properties in and around Soho. I honestly never knew what kind of business was in them … Whatever Humphreys is alleging I'm supposed to have done it didn't make me a rich man. I got my bank statement this morning and my balance is below £170. I'm about fed up with all this. I've had nothing but aggro. I'm changing my phone number and going away. I've had 26 years trying to be a good copper and this is where I finish up.

It was strange that Drury's bank balance was so low. Perhaps the *News of the World* hadn't paid him yet. The writer Iain Sinclair lived in the same street as Drury in Sidcup, Kent, in the 1970s. In his 2007 book *London: City of Disappearances*, which records how the London he knows well has changed, he alludes to this. Sinclair mentions the fact that as Drury's old house was 'the first house in the road to afford an extension' it now 'shows its age when set against today's much slicker extensions'.

Later in that day's *News of the World*, Drury's promised 'Villains I Have Known' article appeared. In it he revealed how he had 'got to know' 'Mad Frankie' Fraser and Great Train Robber Bruce Reynolds, whom we know Drury had tried to bribe in the late 1940s. Drury now said of Reynolds: 'There were no problems. He went quietly.' This was presumably after the teenage Reynolds refused to pay Drury his bribe. Finally, there was Eddie Richardson, who was described as 'polite'. The headline of this second instalment of Drury's 'story' was 'You Don't Catch Villains By Sitting On Your Backside'. But do you catch them by going on holiday with them, eating at the Grosvenor House Hotel, the Talk of the Town and many other places, and taking massive bungs from them? Humphreys may have been an informer, but Drury's biggest 'snout' was undoubtedly his own nose for corruption. And there were still more revelations about Drury to come.

On Tuesday 30 May, Humphreys' solicitor indeed went to see DAC Sheppard of No.1 Area Inspectorate. Humphreys' legal representative gave Sheppard a letter dated 26 May, asking for parts of Humphreys' March 1972 police statements to be withdrawn. A copy of this is in the Met files.

The letter said, regarding Humphreys:

There is no question of his going to Cyprus with Commander Drury in order to look for Biggs. It was purely a vacation which had been arranged some two months previously. The story about looking for Biggs was completely untrue. The Statement that Commander Drury had paid his half share was likewise false. Mr Humphreys wishes to state that he paid for the entire holiday for both Commander and Mrs Drury and the only money which Commander Drury may have expended would have been incidental expenses during the vacation. At no time has Commander, or Mrs Drury, reimbursed Mr Humphreys or Mrs Humphreys, for their share of the money paid to Thomas Cooks. Mr Humphreys wishes it to go on record to the effect that his sole motive in misleading you was in order to assist Mr Drury in his difficulties at the time.

This final sentence was important, as lying to the police in a witnessed statement could have been construed as wasting police time, a criminal offence.

The fact that Humphreys instructed his solicitor to withdraw some of his statements, admitting those parts to be lies, shows that he almost definitely was now telling the truth. What he said in the *News of the World* was one thing, but officially admitting that he had lied was quite another. No. 1 Area Inspectorate did try to get Humphreys to come to the police station and give another statement or be interviewed, repeatedly calling Humphreys' solicitor. But Humphreys proved elusive, going to and fro to Spain apparently.

Another letter to DAC Sheppard from Humphreys' solicitor dated 8 June stated that Humphreys did not want to make a further statement or attend an interview with No. 1 Area Inspectorate. Sheppard concluded his 15 June report into the matter by writing that nobody in his department had believed Humphreys' original story anyway. Sheppard also knew that Humphreys' evidence would not stand up legally. 'It is obvious that Humphreys is a prevaricator, having given one story, he now completely reverses it and in the face of this, no tribunal of any kind could accept his uncorroborated evidence. This report is, therefore, submitted for information and no further action is recommended.'

The report was for the eyes of the Deputy Commissioner, James Hill, who would soon be appointed HM Chief Inspector of Constabulary. Hill would be replaced by James Starritt in July 1972. Commissioner Mark and Deputy Commissioner Starritt would also have to deal with further embarrassment involving the Drugs Squad.

The Drugs Squad was exposed by the *Sunday Times* on 5 November 1972. There had been some concern in Government circles about the Squad for a while, especially about misuse of informants. For example, Kevin Healy, a heroin addict faced with a cannabis charge, had been cultivated as an informer, and instructed to organise a big LSD deal. The Drugs Squad, instead of giving him money for his help, which was normal with informants, gave him some of the LSD seized. Healy had been troubled by this, and went to the police in Oxford, where the deal had taken place, and his concerns were then forwarded to the Home Office. The man in charge of the Drugs Squad was Det. Chief Inspector Victor 'Vic' Kelaher, formerly of the Flying Squad. Apparently, according to Duncan Campbell in *The Underworld*, Kelaher had been the youngest detective chief inspector ever in the history of Scotland Yard.

The final blow for the Drugs Squad, reported in the *Sunday Times*, came when a cannabis dealer named Basil Sands was arrested by Customs and Excise while a large deal was taking place. Sands got a seven-year sentence. But Sands then said that he had been working under the eyes of the Drugs Squad, so that they could catch bigger drug operators. This came less than six months after Drury had spoken very openly about the use of police informants in the *News of the World*. After the *Sunday Times* exposure, five Drugs Squad officers were prosecuted, four getting eighteen-month sentences. However, Kelaher's No.2, Det. Sergeant 'Nobby' Pilcher, got four years because he had run off to Australia. Kelaher, who had already been moved to administrative duties through ill health, was not prosecuted, and resigned from the Met on medical grounds.

The fact that Kelaher escaped punishment is questionable, and raises the possibility of damage limitation after the recent controversies over Drury and Humphreys. Little did the Met Police top brass know that the event which would unravel the complex patchwork of corruption had just occurred, and in an unexpected form.

It was an act of violence, which had taken place in the previous month, which would lead to both the Flying and Dirty Squads being disgraced. And central to that downfall would be Drury's former buddy Jimmy Humphreys. Humphreys could have had 'This Is A Self-Preservation Society', the theme tune to the 1969 Michael Caine likeable-rogue film caper *The Italian Job*, as his personal soundtrack. Rusty Humphreys had just been released from her firearms sentence in Holloway Prison. Enter Peter 'Pooky' Garfath, a former lover of Rusty's.

In late October 1972, Garfath was in the Dauphine Club in Marylebone when he was attacked and seriously slashed by five or six men. The Met files describe Garfath as 'a man with a criminal record' and that Garfath was 'initially reluctant to talk, but eventually fully co-operated naming or describing his attackers'. Humphreys was identified, and some of his henchmen, the motivation seemingly to warn Garfath to stay away from Rusty. Naturally, Humphreys would always deny any involvement in the attack. Humphreys' properties were pulled apart, including his luxurious flat in Dean Street, Soho. Massive amounts of pornography were found. But more ominously for Drury, Moody, Virgo and other members of the Flying Squad and Dirty Squad, Humphreys' diary for 1971 was also seized.

The Met files show that a total of twenty-eight men were pulled in over the attack on Garfath. But when they tried to arrest Humphreys, he was nowhere to be found. He had gone abroad, perhaps tipped off by a bent policeman, whose identity has never been established. As we will shortly see, a Labour Member of Parliament would claim in Parliament that Humphreys had been tipped off.

On 12 February 1973, Humphreys wrote personally to the Deputy Commissioner of the Metropolitan Police, claiming that he had been fitted up by then Det. Chief Inspector (later Superintendent) John Bland. Bland had previously been in the Flying Squad, and was now in the Serious Crime Squad. Humphreys alleged that this fit-up was in retaliation for Humphreys revealing the truth about his relationship with Drury. The Met files reveal that in April, Rusty Humphreys was interviewed by A10. This was in response to a complaint one of Humphreys' porn bookshop managers had made about officers from West End

Central who had 'taken an interest' in the premises. This bookshop had apparently been closed down for a time, had reopened and was trying to build a clientele again.

In the interview, Rusty said that items of property, including her husband's 1971 diary, had been taken in Bland's search, which it had. Rusty also said that she had his 1972 diary in her possession. She added that both diaries contained details of meetings with police officers and corrupt payments to them. Rusty then made a statement, detailing her and Jimmy's associations with corrupt policemen, ranging in rank from constable to commander.

On 15 June, Humphreys was finally arrested in Amsterdam, and detained pending extradition proceedings. Deputy Assistant Commissioner Gilbert Kelland, who as we will see had been chosen by Commissioner Mark to oversee the investigation into pornography and police corruption, travelled there to interview Humphreys. This was achieved with the co-operation of Humphreys' solicitor, on 17 October. Humphreys first agreed to make a tape-recorded or written statement, before changing his mind. Humphreys was obviously playing games as he knew he held the cards of corruption. Drury, Moody and Virgo were the aces. But Humphreys did give a list of names to Kelland, names which he was hoping to sell to the newspapers. Humphreys was finally brought back to Britain on 9 December 1973.

Humphreys stood trial for the assault on Garfath. Other men involved had already been convicted. On 25 April 1974, Humphreys was sentenced to eight years in prison. With nothing left to lose, Humphreys was now extremely dangerous to every corrupt officer he had ever entertained or paid in various ways. For Deputy Assistant Commissioner Kelland of No.4 Area Inspectorate, A10 and Commissioner Mark, it was a godsend. Humphreys was serving up the most witheringly rotten apples in the Metropolitan Police on a self-serving platter.

★ ★ ★

The initial information about Garfath's slashing had come from the Serious Crime Squad, led by Commander Bert Wickstead. Wickstead was known as 'the Gangbuster' and 'the Old Grey Fox'. Wickstead had already brought down some serious gangs in the East End, including the Tibbs, the Dixons, and the Rolls-Royce-driving Philip 'Little Caesar' Jacobs. Now Wickstead would target the Syndicate, so Bernie Silver and 'Big Frank' Mifsud were in his wily sights. In his autobiography *Gangbuster*, Wickstead wrote that during the enquiries into Garfath's slashing, 'we had learned something about vice in the West End, and of the shadowy figures, almost exclusively Maltese [as Silver was a British Jew], who controlled it. We were told that they had become so rich and so powerful that they considered themselves beyond the reach of the law.'

It was estimated that the Syndicate as an entity was raking in around £100,000 a week before the hammer came down. Wickstead had enough evidence to make his move on 4 October 1973 at 1.30 a.m.. At least that was when the raid was planned to take place. But Silver and Mifsud's huge payments to bent police officers was paid back when they were tipped off, allowing them, and others in the next tier down in the Syndicate, to go on the run abroad. Wickstead was frustrated, but decided to enlist the media's help instead of keeping the aborted raid secret, he briefed the press, and an article appeared, calling it 'The Raid That Never Was'.

The raid had not happened because intelligence had been gathered confirming that the vice birds had flown. The idea was that as it had been made public, Silver, Mifsud, and the others would think that the heat was off of them. It was hoped that the top echelons of the Syndicate might think that the target of the Serious Crime Squad was not vice, the Syndicate's speciality, especially prostitution. They might think that Wickstead was targeting pornography. Silver of course had interests in porn too, including with Humphreys at 55 Rupert Street, but the vast majority of his money came from living off of immoral earnings. The system the Syndicate was using was simple but very efficient. The prostitutes worked shifts and paid extortionate rents on between twenty-five and thirty Soho flats farmed by the Syndicate and fronted by others, a conveyor belt of filthy lucre. Wickstead figured that the Syndicate 'directors' would think that porn operators, men such as Humphreys, Mason, Julian, Marandola, etc., were the ones in danger.

The ruse worked, apart from Mifsud, who stayed abroad. The time soon arrived to strike again when Bernie Silver and his long-term girl-friend Dominique 'Kathleen' Ferguson were seen at the Park Tower Hotel in Knightsbridge, on 30 December 1973. Wickstead had them arrested as they left the hotel. They were taken to Limehouse police station, where Wickstead had based the Syndicate investigation, as it was where he felt most in control. It would have been far easier to have taken Silver and Ferguson to a central London police station, but in his memoirs Wickstead explained his motives for transporting them further east. 'I supposed my thinking was partly influenced by the fact that I knew the Syndicate had a few police friends in the area.' The New Year of 1974 wasn't looking good for Silver, although by all accounts he was smooth and unperturbed in early custody. According to James Morton in *Gangland Soho*, an intermediary offered the Serious Crime Squad £35,000 on Silver's behalf, but this was rejected. Old Syndicate habits were slow to die.

Wickstead knew that he couldn't give other members of the Syndicate and its associates time to flee. So the next stop that night was the Scheherazade Club in Soho, which Wickstead called 'the social headquarters of the Syndicate'. Everyone at the club was detained, and treated as suspects until it was known who was who. Other raids were carried out on the homes of other known Syndicate members. In all, some 150 police officers arrested around 170 people that night, including five key Syndicate members. They were all ferried to Limehouse in police vans, Wickstead saying that the station had never been so full. It was an exemplary police operation.

Mifsud was finally tracked down and arrested in Switzerland in a tent on a high-end camping site. After a delay when Mifsud tried to get himself put into a local psychiatric unit to avoid extradition, he would be brought back.

Silver and other leading Syndicate members went to trial at the Old Bailey on 18 September 1974. A key member of the Syndicate, Victor Micallef, had the brother of politician Michael Foot, Sir Dingle Foot, as his defence counsel. It would last over two months, and evidence given claimed that the Perfumed Garden, the Gigi, the Casbah and

Taboo clubs were essentially brothels. A Chinese man named James Hing testified that he and his family had lived in a flat above a Syndicate strip club. He had been asked to move himself and his family out, and when he refused, the stairs leading up to the flat had been chopped away. They had moved. Incredibly, or perhaps not so incredibly, several former policemen gave evidence in support of Silver. Including ex-Commander Frank 'Jeepers' Davies, ex-Head of the Flying Squad, whom Drury had deputised then succeeded, and ex-Det. Sgt Walter Sanderson, later landlord of the White Horse pub in Newburgh Street, Soho. This was allegedly where Silver and Humphreys used to leave policemen their wages. There is no evidence that Sanderson ever knew about this arrangement.

Silver was jailed for six years and received a £30,000 fine, pocket money for Bernie who was found to be purchasing a £27,000 yacht at the time of his arrest. Tony Mangion and Emmanuel Bartolo got five years, Frank Melito four years and Victor Micallef received three years. All the convictions were for conspiracy to live on immoral earnings.

But there was more to come for Silver. Wickstead had been investigating the 25 June 1956 murder of Tommy Smithson. This had taken place when Silver and Mifsud were moving into Soho and attempting to fill the vacuum left by the decline of the Messinas. Smithson had been in their way, it was alleged. Wickstead had tracked down the two assassins, Philip Ellul and Victor Spampinato, going as far as the United States and working with the FBI to do so. Silver was re-arrested, and would be tried for the murder of Smithson.

Meanwhile, 'Big Frank' Mifsud was finally brought back from Switzerland. A photograph shows an uncharacteristically shiny-suited and handcuffed Mifsud, sandwiched between Wickstead and another police officer, leaving a British Airways plane. Mifsud looks crumpled and disillusioned, the fight gone out of him. Wickstead wrote later that Mifsud showed none of the smooth 'grit' of Silver in adversity. Wickstead said that Mifsud told him, 'I've changed,' that family was everything to him now, and that he had given large sums to charity.

The Tommy Smithson murder trial took place in the summer of 1975. Mifsud was acquitted of ordering the murder, but the thorough

Wickstead had other charges prepared with which to nail him. It was a perjury charge relating to the 1966–67 bombings of the Syndicate's Gigi and Keyhole clubs, and the resulting 1967 trial. This involved Tony Cauci and Derek Galea. Mifsud got five years for perjury, but this was quashed on appeal as it was thought that inadmissible evidence had been heard against Mifsud from Galea. Silver was convicted of ordering Smithson's murder, on 8 July 1975, just over nineteen years after Smithson was killed. However, this would also be quashed on appeal on 18 October 1976, as it was considered that 'disreputable witnesses' had appeared.

But Wickstead and the Serious Crime Squad had to all intents and purposes smashed the Syndicate.

★ ★ ★

A week after Humphreys had been arrested in Holland on 15 June 1973, Arthur Lewis, Labour Member of Parliament for the east London constituency of West Ham North, used his parliamentary privilege. Lewis said in the House of Commons that he believed Humphreys had been tipped off to flee, obviously meaning by a bent policeman. Lewis asked for a Home Office statement 'on the investigations by the Metropolitan Police into evidence submitted to them that senior officers of the force have been involved in bribery connected with sexual offences, pornography and drugs'. Lewis was referring to the allegations being made by Humphreys. It cannot be ascertained how Lewis knew this so quickly, but he had also sent a file on the subject of Met Police corruption to Lord Diplock.

A Minister of State from the Home Office, Mr Carlisle, was then forced to make a statement in the House of Commons:

> The Commissioner [Mark] informs me that he has arranged for the allegations which I believe the Hon. Member has in mind to be investigated in accordance with Section 49 of the Police Act 1964, by a Deputy Assistant Commissioner. I have no further comment to make while this investigation is in progress.

It certainly was in progress. The Serious Crime Squad's investigation of the Syndicate had run in parallel with an inquiry into Soho vice and corrupt policemen. The latter was being carried out under the supervision of Deputy Assistant Commissioner Gilbert Kelland of No.4 Area Inspectorate, and had begun in early 1973. Kelland's team was comprised of Commander Steventon, also of No.4, Det. Chief Supt Howard and Det. Chief Inspector Hay of A10, and Det. Chief Supt Williams of 'N' Division. With access to the Met files and Kelland's three major reports, which included five statements made by Jimmy Humphreys and wider police enquiries, we can see for the first time in detail what he found. This includes hitherto undisclosed revelations, which rooted out the huge corruption in the Flying Squad and Dirty Squad at last.

The pressure was on Commissioner Mark, and Kelland and his men. Martin Short put it succinctly in *Lundy: The Destruction of Scotland Yard's Finest Detective*: 'If Drury and his far more corrupt colleagues were to get off scot-free, then Mark and the senior officers spearheading his anti-corruption purge would have egg not just on their epaulettes, but all over their faces' – although this author disagrees with the view that Drury was less corrupt than his colleagues. In regards to his corruption connected to Soho, yes. The sums that Drury took were less than Moody and Virgo, but it has to be remembered that Drury was only head of the Flying Squad for just over fifteen months, with the final seven weeks of that on suspension. Moody and Virgo had enjoyed real autonomous power for far longer. But when Drury's nasty handiwork in the Luton Post Office Murder case is taken into account, his corruption lowers him into a new league of depravity.

Though there were men of bravery and integrity serving in the Flying Squad, Drury and, to a much lesser extent, another Flying Squad officer, would soil its name as the 1970s progressed. Conversely, Patrick Gibbins, known as 'Pat the Cat' within the Sweeney, is a reminder of the kind of man that Fred Wensley would have approved of all those years before in 1919 when he designed the Flying Squad.

Born in north London in 1930, Gibbins was active against many London gangs, including the Richardsons. He won the British Empire Medal twice, the first for the capture of the armed robber Walter Probyn in 1964. He won the second in 1970, when he chased a gang armed with iron bars and ammonia. Gibbins managed to land a punch on one of the gang, but was attacked with an iron bar in response. He suffered a serious head wound and this forced his retirement. This incident took place when Commander Frank 'Jeepers' Davies, Silver's courtroom referee, was Head of the Flying Squad, with Drury his No.2.

Gibbins earned fourteen commendations, one more than Drury, as well as nine commendations from Judges at the Old Bailey, and one from the Director of Public Prosecutions. Patrick Gibbins died at the age of eighty-three on 25 May 2013.

6

THE SWEENEY GET NICKED

Bexley Lane, Sidcup, Kent, 28 February 1976, dawn

WHAT A LOAD of aggro, a palaver, Drury must have thought when they finally came for him. Out of the Met and the Flying Squad for almost four years, with a pension still to show for years of service and corruption, and this is what you get. What a fucking liberty, he might have said, coming for a man impromptu, waking up the missus and before his prized sideburns have been properly coiffed. Making him puff down the stairs like the dad of one of the toerags he used to chase for his legitimate and illegitimate living. It beggared all kinds of belief, this assault on his newly extended castle. But he was in the shit now no question. They didn't come for you like this unless they meant business. He had to brazen it out as always, he surely knew.

Do they know about the Luton job? If so, I'm proper stuffed. Don't worry dear, I've done nuthin' wrong, have a cup of tea, calm down – I was only doin' my job … I'm being arrested. There's the press outside, a right fucking mickey-take this is, a 21 carat rib-tickler, thirteen commendations and they call in the muck-sheets. It's Saturday, so just in time for the Sunday papers, bleedin' hell. Now the neighbours are all waking up. Give me a blanket, you tosser. I was on the beat before you were even a possibility. I was Head of the Sweeney, son.

★ ★ ★

A photograph of Drury cowering under a blanket like a serial killer or child molester was indeed in the next day's *News of the World* – the very paper that had bought the two-week serialisation of Drury's 'story' in 1972. The press had been informed. It was good to be seen to be cleaning up the Met, positive coverage for a change. The writer Iain Sinclair, who lived on Bexley Lane where Drury resided with Joan and family, later remembered seeing the commotion in the street that day, writing, 'Fleet Street swamped our road, in the 1970s, to record this event.'

But not only Drury was taken. It was a series of raids, twelve officers and former officers in total, ex-Commander Drury and two other Flying Squad officers, Virgo from Central Office, and Moody and seven others from the Dirty Squad. It would be a series of Magistrates' Court appearances now. As shown in the Prologue, at one appearance Drury was confronted by the brother of David Cooper, who Drury had framed for the Luton Post Office Murder. The Dirty Squad went to trial first, the Sweeney having to wait a little longer until Humphreys spewed out all of his allegations. In fact, Humphreys would also implicate Moody and the Dirty Squad in a big way. But then so would John 'Eric' Mason and other pornographers, as we will see. In December 1974, Deputy Assistant Commissioner Kelland had found out during his investigation that Mason was a serious player in Soho, far bigger than Humphreys, according to some.

Moody had been informed of this through the whispering Met grass. Knowing that Mason knew enough to bring down a large part of the Dirty Squad, Moody and fellow corrupt Dirty Squad officer Det. Chief Inspector George Fenwick met Mason and his driver, Ron 'the Dustman' Davey at the Serpentine in Hyde Park. They warned Mason to leave the country. Mason took the advice, but when Moody continued to receive tip-offs that the No.4 Inspectorate/A10 inquiry was intensifying, Moody went further. He visited Mason on Guernsey, where Mason was living. According to Barry Cox et al., in their 1977 book *The Fall of Scotland Yard*, Moody threatened Mason, but this backfired. Fearing for his life, Mason decided to work with Deputy Assistant Commissioner Kelland. They didn't call Moody 'Wicked Bill' for nothing.

In fact, Mason's driver Ron 'the Dustman' Davey had a colourful history of his own. Davey would also give evidence to Kelland's team about Moody and the Dirty Squad, and testify against Moody at his trial. Moody would say in court that he had no idea that Davey was a pornographer, but Wicked Bill would be discredited. Davey really had been a dustman in the repressed 1950s, but from 1957 he'd had a sideline, asking women at the Surrey Nudist Club to pose for dirty photos. Soon he was selling a large amount of photos every week. The *News of the World* reported that in 1960 Davey had been arrested in his darkroom with 2,468 porn photos, and at other premises 15,000 porn negatives and 15,000 dirty photos were found. Davey got six months in prison for publishing (i.e. selling) 744 improper photos of men and 105 of women.

Davey told the police in 1975 that he first met Det. Chief Supt Moody at a party thrown by another pornographer, at Trader Vic's restaurant in the Hilton Hotel. He also associated with Det. Inspector Cyril Jones of the Dirty Squad. Moody and Jones were Freemasons, as was Drury incidentally. Davey said, 'Bill [Moody] introduced me into his Lodge ... All were Masonic functions at which I was a guest. Normally present were Bill Moody, Cyril Jones and two other police officers and our wives.' Actually, the two most senior officers of No.4 Inspectorate investigating the corruption in the corruption in the Flying and Dirty Squads, DAC Gilbert Kelland and Commander Ronald Steventon, were also in the Brotherhood. They were both members of the Manor of St James Lodge.

There was a famous heatwave that summer of 1976. But Drury, Moody, Virgo and the other Flying and Dirty Squad officers had more to sweat about than most. In wider society, the government battled to save the car manufacturer British Leyland, and employment rights for women improved. In sport, it was the year when James Hunt and Niki Lauda fought it out for the Formula One motor-racing World Championship, with Lauda crashing and being horrifically burnt, then resuming the wheel after a brief period of recuperation. Hunt won the title. It was the summer when the England cricket captain Tony Grieg said that he would make the formidable and touring West Indies side grovel. Actually, the West Indies would beat England in every test match.

But for those twelve Metropolitan Police former and suspended elite Squad officers, cricket was far from their minds. They had all either been suspended or retired in 1973–74 as we shall see. Except Drury, of course, who had resigned in May 1972. The length of time that it had taken the Met to catch up with them, Moody's intervention to keep Mason quiet, and the information that Drury, Moody and Virgo especially would have had passed to them from police contacts, would have left them in no doubt that they were in serious trouble. Experienced police officers, they knew that Commissioner Mark would make an example of them. In fact, Mark had taken the pornography brief away from the Dirty Squad and the CID and given it to uniform in the form of 'A' Division and Divisional Commanders in October 1972. This shows that Mark knew how corrupt the Dirty Squad was, before he ordered Kelland to start his inquiry in early 1973.

For the guilty police officers, it was just a case of how much the Director of Public Prosecutions could prove in order to prosecute.

★ ★ ★

The allegations which would bring down the corrupt members of the Flying Squad, Dirty Squad and ex-Commander Virgo of Central Office would largely come from the pornographers – John 'Eric' Mason, Jimmy Humphreys, Evan 'Big Jeff' Phillips and Gerald Citron, although many others also gave evidence too.

The members of the Flying Squad concerned were of course ex-Commander Kenneth Drury, Det. Inspector Alistair Ingram and a detective inspector, who should not be named here as he was acquitted; The Dirty Squad: ex-Det. Chief Supt Moody, ex-Det. Inspector David Jones, known by his middle name Cyril, ex-Det. Chief Inspector George Fenwick, Det. Inspector Edward O'Hanlon, Det. Inspector Leslie Alton, Det. Inspector Rodney Tilley, ex-Det. Constable Bernard Brown, ex-Det. Constable Michael Chamberlain, plus some others, who would only be arrested later as the result of further police inquiries. As already stated, the Dirty Squad would come to trial first. Actually, the corruption was so rife that two trials were required.

John 'Eric' Mason began opening up to Kelland in April 1976, the same month he received a £25,000 fine for the possession of obscene publications. It is also very likely that Moody's arrest, although he was on bail, made Mason feel able to divulge the deep wrongdoings of the Dirty Squad. 'Wicked Bill' could hardly make a move against him while in the spotlight. Mason was notorious in Soho as a pornographer and had the nickname 'God', and this shows his true power and reputation. Mason told Kelland that he had started paying the Dirty Squad £60 a month in 1953, twenty-three years earlier. By the late 1960s, Mason was paying £250 a month. His monthly payment in 1971, the peak of Soho pornography, was a massive £1,000.

He also alleged that he had been able to go into the basement of Holborn police station and have his pick of the pornography confiscated from unflavoured dealers. He had paid between £500 and £1,000 for that privilege. The Dirty Squad even provided him with the Squad tie to wear, so that his presence at the station was less questionable. Added to this, Det. Chief Inspector George Fenwick, who would take over the Dirty Squad from Moody for a time, had acted as an editorial advisor on his magazines since 1972. Fenwick had taken over after the death of an ex-Det. Supt, who had provided that same service for some time, for £10 a week. Therefore, members of the Dirty Squad were not only receiving illicit payments from pornographers but even helping one produce his material. That police function was not stated in the Obscene Publications Act of 1959 nor 1964.

Deputy Assistant Commissioner Kelland's report of 3 December 1974 in the Met files deals first with Jimmy Humphreys' allegations against Dirty Squad officers. Ex-Det. Chief Supt Moody, former Head of the Dirty Squad, was first to be interviewed, as he was 'the most senior officer involved who was still serving'. Moody had been transferred to Division on 23 October 1972, as part of Commissioner Mark's restructuring. Moody was suspended from duty on 14 June 1974, and retired on an ill-health pension on 30 July 1974 whilst still under suspension. Moody lived in Weybridge, Surrey.

Humphreys claimed that he had first tried to get a porn licence from Moody in 1964, but as Kelland noted, this must have been wrong, as Moody didn't join the Dirty Squad until 1965. Humphreys then stated that it wasn't until 1969, after the meeting at the Criterion restaurant we witnessed earlier, that Moody relented and sold him the license for £10,000 to open up the bookshop at 55 Rupert Street, in a 50/50 partnership with Bernie Silver. Moody had been interviewed about these allegations in June 1974, and had 'adamantly denied receiving money from either Silver or Humphreys'. Kelland continued about Moody:

> There was however conclusive evidence of his close personal association with other persons involved with pornography. As the result of arrangements, made by him, his daughter honeymooned in July 1971 free of charge in an apartment in Malta owned by a convicted pornographer. Moody acquired, allegedly by cash purchase without receipts, an almost new Lancia motor car from yet another convicted pornographer, and there is evidence in direct conflict with Moody's claim that he was unaware of the man's conviction and pornographic trade investment.

Like Moody, Det. Inspector Cyril Jones had joined the Dirty Squad in 1965, specifically 5 September 1965. Jones had been transferred to 'F' Division on 14 June 1971, and was suspended on 5 April 1974. He had been a detective sergeant when he was involved in corruption on the Dirty Squad. Jones lived in Sunbury-on-Thames. Kelland wrote of Jones:

> He was alleged by some of those dealing in pornography to be 'Moody's right hand man' and the collector for Moody of corrupt payments. It may be coincidental that on his promotion to Det. Inspector on 25 February 1974, he was transferred to 'F' Division, and again served with Mr Moody. It is a point of interest that he is now [December 1974] living in the house formerly owned by Mr Moody in 1967 while both were serving with C.1 Obscene Publications Squad.

Kelland also makes reference to a search of Humphreys' shop and 'the subsequent meeting and payment of £100 at Waterloo Railway Station. These allegations are denied by both Moody and Jones.' Jones would also be the subject of allegations made by 'Big Jeff' Phillips. But perhaps the most incredible new revelation in the Met files about Jones is his involvement with Det. Chief Inspector Fenwick and Det. Constable Michael Chamberlain, all of the Dirty Squad, in a car-hire business.

> Kelland: During the course of this enquiry it was learned that Jones was concerned with two other officers in running a car hire firm trading under the registered business names of Coulsdon Car Hire from premises at Station Approach, Coulsdon, Surrey and Tolworth Car Hire at 450 Ewell Road, Tolworth, Surrey. The officers are said to have acquired the business during April 1973 and to have jointly paid in the region of £9,000 in cash. The sources from which they obtained such a large cash sum are open to conjecture.

Coincidentally, there had been a criminal trial in 1972 involving a car-dealer named Leslie Payne, who also lived in Coulsdon, Surrey, and James Moor and John Hutton, both car dealers too. The three were on trial for conspiracy to obstruct and pervert the course of justice, and for a charge of embracery. The prosecution alleged that 'between £1,000 and £2,000' had been given to Mr Payne to fix the trial of four men. Payne alleged through his counsel in court that he had paid money to seven police officers. He named Drury and Leonard 'Nipper' Read, as well as five more junior officers. No evidence was ever found to substantiate these allegations.

Det. Chief Inspector Fenwick had been in the Dirty Squad from 15 December 1969, succeeding Moody as Head, until he was transferred to 'V' Division on 3 January 1972. Fenwick was suspended on 5 April 1974, and as of December 1974 had refused to answer any questions put to him. Fenwick lived in East Ewell, Surrey. At the trial, three ex-Dirty Squad officers would testify that Fenwick would put money in their pockets on Friday nights when they were new to the Squad, thus enmeshing them.

> Kelland on Fenwick: Humphreys claims a close and corrupt association with him from the time Fenwick took active charge of the Pornography

Squad, an appointment made by Commander Virgo. A degree of corroboration is provided by Evan John [Big Jeff] Phillips ... Fenwick was
involved ... in the purchase and running of the car hire firms.

The hand of Wally Virgo the fixer is seen again, fixing the appoint-
ment of a bent officer, just as Virgo had had an honest officer, Det.
Chief Supt Lambert, removed from the *Times* Inquiry and replaced by
'Wicked Bill' Moody.

Det. Constable Michael Chamberlain, the third of the Dirty Squad
officers involved in the car-hire business, had arrived in the Squad
on 24 August 1970. He stayed with it temporarily when its powers
were devolved to uniform branch in October 1972. Chamberlain
voluntarily resigned from the Met on 5 August 1973. Chamberlain
lived in Biggin Hill, Kent. Kelland wrote that Humphreys claimed
that he only had two meetings with Chamberlain, when corrupt
payments were made. Also that Det. Sgt O'Hanlon had also been
present on both occasions. Edward O' Hanlon had joined the Dirty
Squad as a detective sergeant on 24 May 1971, and remained there
after devolvement, until he was promoted to detective inspector on
5 February 1973. He lived in Cobham, Surrey, and was suspended on
3 May 1974.

Kelland on O'Hanlon: He was allegedly introduced to Humphreys by
Det Chief Inspector Fenwick and subsequently received regular monthly
and miscellaneous payments from him. Their association began shortly
after he was posted to COC1 [Dirty Squad] when his name and telephone number appear in Humphreys' diaries and continued well beyond
the time when publicity was given to the Drury affair. O'Hanlon had
dealings with Gerald Conrad Citron, a pornographer ... Suffice it to say
at this stage that Citron was one of those arrested by the Serious Crime
Squad in January 1973. He had been previously arrested by uniform
officers on 19 July 1972 when stopped in the street whilst in possession
of a considerable quantity of pornographic material. O'Hanlon took
charge of the enquiry, and it is alleged he substituted the hard pornography material for relatively soft porn magazines, in an attempt to lessen

the gravity of the offence. The corrupt dealings to protect Citron by O'Hanlon and other officers were allegedly still continuing when Citron was arrested by the Serious Crime Squad.

Humphreys also made an allegation about how the corrupt payments to police were collected sometimes, according to Kelland:

> Humphreys, whilst in custody in Holland, through his wife, said that [name redacted] a convicted pornographer, was a collector of money from bookshops for police. The man would not admit this, but enquiries revealed that he lived in a house owned by [name redacted] to whom he was known as a convicted pornographer.

The obvious inference here is that the house in which the man lived was owned by a serving or former police officer. In another report in the Met files, as we shall see, it is confirmed that the house was owned by an ex-detective inspector.

There were claims made by Humphreys against several other Dirty Squad officers, but the offences were minor and they were not prosecuted. Then there were the allegations made by Evan 'Big Jeff' Phillips, a former accountant. Phillips had undoubtedly used his numerical skills in building his porn empire, which was largely in blue movies. Phillips had been caught when the premises storing his pornography in Surrey was discovered. Phillips committed suicide at the age of 33, apparently because of a failed love affair, not his porn downfall, although he was broke at the time of his death. Therefore, Phillips would not give evidence against the Dirty Squad at the trials, but he did speak to Kelland after he got eighteen months in prison and fines in January 1974. Kelland states that Phillips described himself as 'a property speculator' and he had built up a substantial property portfolio. This included the flat in Sloane Square which fellow vice operator Charles Julian lived in for a while. But these properties were presumably all mortgaged.

Kelland wrote that some of Phillips' and Humphreys' claims corroborated each other. These related to Moody, Jones, O'Hanlon and Fenwick. Added to this, there were allegations against ex-Det. Inspector

Leslie Alton, who had joined the Dirty Squad in late 1966. Alton transferred to 'Z' Division on 2 February 1968, before being returned to uniform on unrelated grounds. He retired on pension on 31 August 1974. Alton lived in Cheam, Surrey. Phillips claimed that Alton was 'fully aware of the monthly payments' Phillips made to the police and was 'a party to them'. In fact, at Alton's trial, a Det. Constable Frank Andrews, who joined the Dirty Squad in 1965 like Moody, and left in 1968 like Alton, would give evidence against Alton. Andrews alleged that Alton had ordered him to collect weekly payments from pornographers and then share it out. Andrews also said that almost everyone in the Dirty Squad had new cars and plush homes.

Phillips also implicated ex-Det. Constable Bernard Brown, who joined the Dirty Squad on 9 November 1967. Brown served there until 23 November 1970, when he was transferred to Division. After thirteen years in the Met, he voluntarily resigned on 5 November 1972. Phillips alleged that Brown, who lived in Dorking, Surrey, was also concerned in the monthly payment collections. Then there was ex-Det. Inspector Rodney Tilley, who had served as a detective sergeant in the Dirty Squad from 19 February 1968 to 24 May 1971, when he moved to Division. Tilley retired on an ill-health pension on 25 July 1974, after serving in the Met for seventeen years. Phillips alleged that Tilley had also been present at the corrupt payment meetings. Additionally, Phillips said that a detective inspector on the Dirty Squad, whose name is redacted, had declined the offer of monthly payments, but was 'well-aware of the corrupt arrangements which had existed'.

The pornographer Gerald Citron had no previous convictions, according to the Met files, until he was arrested by the Serious Crime Squad in January 1973. Citron ended up being fined £50,000 for his involvement in pornography. Citron's allegations against the Dirty Squad dated from early 1970. Kelland states: 'His statement tells a story of monthly payments, connivance to avoid prosecution, seeking police aid to collect his debts, and social entertainment of officers akin to and in part corroboration of the accounts of Humphreys and Phillips.' This corroboration related to Fenwick, Chamberlain and O'Hanlon, and another officer whose name is redacted. Allegedly, either this officer or O'Hanlon 'briefed' Citron on what to say when he gave evidence to Lord Longford's self-financed inquiry into vice. Citron also alleged that one officer, name redacted, who was awaiting trial on unrelated corruption charges, was involved in monthly payments. This officer had allegedly been paid £500 to prevent Citron being prosecuted, and had been in the Dirty Squad from June 1969 until August 1970. Citron would go to the United States, resist attempts to extradite him, and not give evidence in court.

Next was ex-Det. Sgt Peter Fisher, who was in the Dirty Squad from 6 May 1968 until he was transferred to Division on 5 June 1972. Fisher was suspended from duty on 3 May 1974. Kelland:

He took over the monthly payments after being introduced by [name redacted]. There is evidence that Fisher sought to conceal Citron's involvement with hard pornography in reports he sent to Constabularies, concerning the man and these are the grounds for his suspension from duty.

Citron alleged that a detective sergeant, who was in the Dirty Squad from December 1969 until July 1973, was also involved. The officer was not suspended in December 1974. His name was not redacted, but as no evidence can be found of his prosecution he will not be named here.

He was one of the officers who searched Citron's vehicle in May of 1971, and took possession of a quantity of pornography and blue films which Citron, after he had signed a disclaimer, heard had found their way on to the market.

★ ★ ★

Humphreys also made allegations against ex-Commander Wallace 'Wally' Virgo, in charge of Central Office. Ironically, on 26 April 1972, Virgo had been transferred to No. 4 Area Inspectorate, Kelland's unit, the very one now investigating him. Virgo resigned on pension on 14 March 1973.

Kelland on Virgo in December 1974: In October 1974 he suffered a severe heart attack, is still convalescing, and has declined to be interviewed. He has sent a formal letter in which he absolutely denies receiving any money or gifts from Humphreys. According to Humphreys, they first met in 1969, and although the very first meeting cannot be verified, there is evidence that at a subsequent meeting they had a discussion over the possible assault of a prison governor, as described by Humphreys. Humphreys' claim to have attended what he describes as 'Buffalo Lodge Ladies Night' at the Criterion Restaurant [the December 1969 meeting detailed earlier] has been proved, but there is no corroboration of his meeting there with Mr Virgo and the resultant conversation which led him to embark on his meeting with Moody. If Humphreys' story is true, Virgo received substantial payments from the joint 'porn empire' of Humphreys and Silver.

Kelland's report also details the allegations made by Humphreys against Det. Superintendent John Bland. This regarded Humphreys' arrest for the violent assault on Peter 'Pooky' Garfath, and the investigations of the Serious Crime Squad, under Commander Wickstead. Bland had been on the Flying Squad until 3 January 1972, when he was transferred to Division. He had then moved to the Serious Crime Squad on 15 May 1972, where he investigated the Garfath slashing and searched Humphreys' apartment, finding his 1971 diary in a wall safe. Bland had joined 'A' Division on 15 April 1974.

Kelland on Humphreys' allegation: The complaint against Bland falls into an entirely different category … [Humphreys] suggests that £3,000 was paid to Bland, through a licensee and former Detective Sergeant acting as a middleman, as a joint payment by Silver and himself to influence the major enquiry being made by the Serious Crime Squad into their activities. It is always possible that Silver has defrauded Humphreys of the sum of £1,500 … From an early stage in Bland's enquiry it was realised that through the publicity over Humphreys and Drury's association, Humphreys would claim, as he now does, that he was the victim of a 'backlash' from that affair. He attempts to justify this viewpoint by pointing out that Bland was a Detective Inspector under Drury on the Flying Squad, but he admits that at no time during his association with Drury did he meet Mr Bland. Bland acted with the knowledge and under directions from his senior officer and on all the evidence obtained to date behaved perfectly properly.

No action was ever taken against Bland over Humphreys' allegations, and nothing proved. It does appear that Humphreys was trying to wriggle out of his conviction for the assault on Garfath by implicating Bland.

Kelland's 3 December 1974 report is also very enlightening about the relationship between Humphreys, his porn suppliers and his corrupt police friends. This revelation regards Pieter Mulder, a Dutchman aged 39, who was living in Germany at the end of 1974. Mulder had been arrested by the Dirty Squad in July 1972, just three months before it was devolved to uniform. The Mulder case implicates O'Hanlon and Chamberlain of the Dirty Squad, and another five officers whose names are redacted. One of these officers was a detective constable on the Dirty Squad, who had been suspended and acquitted over perjury in the Drug Squad trial involving ex-Det. Chief Inspector Victor Kelaher, mentioned earlier. The officer resigned voluntarily on 5 May 1974 and moved to Australia.

Mulder acted as an agent or middleman for Humphreys in the collection of porn consignments from abroad. Mulder collected fifty-five boxes of porn for Humphreys in this transaction. Humphreys had gone to Holland to arrange the deal with Mulder's boss, and Mulder was also bringing in fifteen boxes for another pornographer. For his fifty-five boxes, Humphreys had agreed to pay the pornography company Rodox Ltd (spelt 'Rodex' by Kelland) in Copenhagen, Denmark, £4,000 wholesale. This was described by Kelland as 'just a normal routine pornographic deal'. But the retail price for Humphreys was enormous. Police enquiries had ascertained that each box, with each magazine inside selling for £5 in Soho, had a retail value of £2,250. So Humphreys could make £157,500 from his £4,000 investment, plus other overheads, including Mulder and his boss, of course. No wonder Jimmy didn't mind paying his police pals their protection money.

But the transaction wasn't all it appeared.

Kelland on Humphreys: Although he did not make a direct confession, it can be deduced from entries in his diary as well as from absolutely reliable information received, that Humphreys informed Det. Sergeant O'Hanlon about Mulder. As a result Mulder was followed by police and the garage where he had temporarily stored his 55 boxes was located. A search warrant was obtained and as he was about to move the load to affect delivery to Humphreys, Mulder was arrested and all the property was seized. He was taken to a local police station where initially 34 boxes of pornography were shown as being found in his van. For some reason, for which conflicting explanations have been given, this figure was subsequently altered to 30, on some, but not all, of the police official records.

As Kelland pointed out, this meant that 25 boxes, worth some £56,200 retail, went straight to Humphreys. Mulder appeared in court the next day and his £2,000 bail was supplied by the ever-so-generous Humphreys. Mulder escaped to Dublin, as arranged with Humphreys, on a false passport. It showed what cunning and connivance with bent police officers could do.

★ ★ ★

Humphreys also made allegations against other Flying Squad officers, who were never prosecuted. Humphreys mentioned a detective chief inspector of the Flying Squad, whose name is redacted. Deputy Assistant Commissioner Kelland said, 'He became involved with Humphreys solely through serving with Commander Drury. He was wined, dined and entertained on a few occasions but always in company with Mr Drury under whose directions he claims he was acting.' Kelland goes on to say that this man, like another detective chief superintendent of the Flying Squad, had confirmed the false story about Drury and Humphreys looking for Ronnie Biggs in Cyprus 'out of a misguided sense of loyalty to their Commander'. There was also an ex-detective inspector of the Flying Squad, whose name is redacted, whom

Humphreys said he had had a close association with, which continued after the officer left the Met. Humphreys said that he had a high regard for this man and liked him, and was reluctant to talk about him. But Humphreys said the man ony received 'a drink on some occasions'.

Two other allegations made by Humphreys about Flying Squad officers whose names are redacted relate to the pornographer Charles Julian, whom we met earlier. When Julian was arrested for 'possessing and uttering' a forged $100 bill, Humphreys said that he had acted as a middleman. Humphreys said he had used his influence with police to get Julian bail, and to hide the fact that Julian had other counterfeit notes too. Humphreys alleged that he paid the Flying Squad officers £1,000 for ensuring this was achieved, and that Julian was supposed to pay him back in pornography, which Humphreys would of course have sold.

> Kelland: 'This aspect has already been investigated in some detail and it is apparent that Julian's extensive US criminal record was not made known to the Central Criminal Court when he was fined £1,000 on each of the two counts of his indictment.'

Kelland concluded that there was no evidence that the two Flying Squad officers had received the details of Julian's US record from the FBI. But the FBI's records showed that his US rap sheet had been sent. Met Police officers had gone to see Julian in the US since, but he had changed his mind about being interviewed. Humphreys also implicated a detective inspector of the Flying Squad, who was consequently suspended and went on trial. This officer would be acquitted, so he will not be named or the allegations against him explored here.

Another detective inspector of the Flying Squad, Alistair Ingram, had significant allegations made against him by Humphreys. Ingram was posted to 'C' Division on 23 November 1964, on being promoted to the rank of detective sergeant. Later in the 1960s, he would be assigned to the protection of a witness in an important trial of that decade. The name of this trial is redacted, but the emphasis given to it infers that it was a major trial. In 1970, when Drury arrived in the Flying Squad, to become Head at the beginning of the following year, Ingram, by now a detective inspector, served under Drury. The allegations that Humphreys made against Ingram can be revealed here for the first time in detail. These allegations were dealt with by Commander Ronald Steventon, Kelland's second in command on the A10/No.4 Area Inspectorate inquiry. Steventon submitted a report to Kelland on 7 May 1975. Drury was jointly concerned in some of the allegations made against Ingram, but Drury was far more corrupt than Ingram, and he will be dealt with separately next.

Humphreys claimed that he met Ingram for the first time in early 1960. But we know that Humphreys was serving a prison sentence between March 1958 and October 1962, so this is incorrect. Steventon stated, 'I attach no particular significance to this and it is a minor error in a period of Humphreys' story for which he has no diary entry to refer to.'

It also seems that Ingram worked under a detective chief inspector, name redacted, but also of the Flying Squad (of whose conduct Steventon had no criticism), on an investigation into allegations against Inspector Leslie Alton of the Dirty Squad. As both Alton and Ingram would in time be convicted for corruption, this is farcical. But as Steventon points out, 'This was prior to the advent of A10 and it was the usual practice for C8 officers [Flying Squad] to investigate allegations against C1 officers [Dirty Squad] and the reverse usually applied.' As both the Flying Squad and Dirty Squad were riddled with corruption, this shows how complaints could potentially have been swept aside or not properly investigated.

In March 1970, a man whose name is redacted, whose identity has been worked out but cannot be named for legal reasons, was in custody for an assault on his wife which had caused actual bodily harm. The wife was interviewed by Hampshire Constabulary police officers about the assault. She told them that her husband was the owner of two porn bookshops at 37 and 69 Berwick Street in Soho, and that he had been paying 'regular monthly cash sums' to Alton, for 'a licence to trade without police interference'. But 'no evidence was found to support the allegation, and [her husband] and his associates strongly denied it and the complaint was regarded as "not substantiated".'

In fact, Humphreys owned the lease at 37 Berwick Street of course.

One of Humphreys' allegations against Ingram was that he paid Ingram £50 'for keeping him informed of developments' on the case, as Ingram was investigating Alton. Humphreys also said that Bernie Silver 'was also concerned in the progress of this enquiry and made arrangements for [the woman's husband] to be seen and told what to say when interviewed'. Reference is then made to a courier (name redacted) who worked for Silver and who had been interviewed by A10, but since died. The courier claimed that he had visited the woman's husband in Winchester Prison. Steventon on the courier: 'He was closely associated with Silver at that time and the explanation he gave for the visit savoured of the lame excuse it is now known to be.'

The woman's husband was also interviewed, but he 'firmly stuck to his denials of complicity or indeed knowledge of any corruption connected with pornography and would not make a written statement'. But soon after, he was arrested for pornography dealing, received a twelve-month prison sentence, suspended for two years, and was fined £5,000. He left London and moved to the Isle of Wight. A10 approached him again for an interview, and he said he would speak to them, but was worried about facing prosecution himself. When A10 gained his trust, the man gave a long statement, admitted the corrupt payments story alleged by his wife. The man's statement corroborated some of Humphreys' allegations, with minor variations. In the eyes of Steventon, it also provided confirmation that Humphreys and Silver had an interest in the enquiry against Alton. Also that Ingram was keeping Humphreys and Silver informed of developments and that the man had been coached what to say when interviewed.

Steventon makes reference to an interview with a collector of money from bookshops for police, whose name is redacted. But Steventon states that he was living in a house owned by a former detective inspector, and that this man was still 'seemingly loyal to his former police associates'. The two facts may well be connected.

The man had not been specifically questioned at that time about allegations made by the man who had given his statement on the Isle of Wight about corrupt payments. The man had implicated (name redacted) in that process as the collector. Steventon writes that in his statement, this convicted pornographer who had allegedly assaulted his wife had said that he had paid £250 'at the instigation' of the courier for the help given by Ingram and the other police officer. Humphreys claimed that the man 'had no knowledge of Ingram's duplicity … and there is no tangible evidence to connect him with any impropriety', during their investigation into Alton. But Steventon concludes that the courier's corroboration of Humphreys' allegation against Ingram in this respect would be vital.

Ex-Commander Wally Virgo then enters the story once again. It relates to an alleged meeting between Virgo and Humphreys, in which Ingram was not directly involved. But Virgo had apparently seen the case papers about the investigation into Alton conducted by Ingram and the other officer. Virgo had been in overall charge, and Drury, Moody, Alton and Ingram's superior officer. Humphreys said that Virgo had 'considered Ingram had not been fairly dealt with'. Humphreys alleged that this led him to 'give the motor car to Ingram'. Later in the report, this car is said to have been a Singer Vogue Estate. Enquiries had confirmed that Humphreys had become the registered owner of the Singer Vogue Estate on 23 August 1971, and that on 1 February 1972, incidentally shortly after Humphreys returned from his holiday with Drury, the car's ownership was transferred to Ingram's wife.

Humphreys' 1972 diary had shown an entry marked 'Vogue Service' on 2 September 1972, and Ingram said that he had bought the car in December 1971. Ingram had not insured the car until 15 March 1972. Ingram blamed his wife for the delay in registering and insuring the car. Humphreys claimed that he had 'allowed the existing tax and insurance on the vehicle to run after he passed the car over'.

Steventon: Humphreys valued the car at about £800 and alleges he gave it to Ingram with no question of payment solely because he was mindful that he had not been generous over his help in the [pornographer's] complaint. Ingram denies this and claims he purchased the car for £900 in cash, which he borrowed from his friend [redacted] and he obtained no receipt. At the time he was interviewed Ingram promised to provide a copy of his bank statement which he claimed would show a withdrawal of £600 as a part payment to [redacted]. He did not produce it and the whole matter of the loan by [redacted] and the seemingly haphazard repayment, without any form of record, is difficult to believe.

Humphreys also alleged that he had paid for renovations to Ingram's house. A carpenter and a 'street trader', employees of Humphreys, had been interviewed and confirmed that they had carried out work at Ingram's address. Court reports show that Ingram lived in Esher, Surrey. Humphreys had paid his employees' wages for their labour on Ingram's house. This work, the fitting of a new bathroom, had been carried out in October 1971, and Steventon said, 'Ingram has produced invoices for various materials.'

There is also mention of a 49-year-old businessman, the managing director of a security company. This man was present at a 'promotion party' where both Ingram and Humphreys were also present. According to the businessman, the venue was planned to be the Regent Palace Hotel, but this had been changed at the last minute. Humphreys had insisted on paying the bill, unsurprisingly. The businessman claimed when interviewed that he put £15–20 on the plate, and that Ingram did the same, and others then followed suit. Steventon wrote that there was no doubt that the businessman was at the party, but that Humphreys could not remember him being there. Reading between the lines, it can be said that this businessman was very likely the same man who Ingram claimed had lent him the money to buy the Singer Vogue Estate car. This man had also backed up Ingram's account of events.

Steventon explained that he had had some difficulty arranging an interview with the businessman, 'as he had suffered a mild heart attack which confined him to bed, immediately he learned of our desire to see him'. Steventon then gave his impression of the businessman and the interview:

He is to all outward appearance an eminently respectable businessman and his word is likely to be accepted in preference to that of Humphreys, but nevertheless I was left with a strong suspicion that [redacted] was recounting a well- rehearsed story. He is acquainted with a number of senior police officers, all of whom regard him most highly.

Elsewhere in the report, Steventon added about the businessman, 'It is a strange coincidence that [redacted] provides such vital evidence over the two most damaging allegations which arise against Ingram.' Steventon assessed that Ingram had had little influence on the 'West End scene', meaning Soho, as he was in the Flying Squad. But he did have influence in stopping police interference, and so was attractive to Humphreys, who was also of course courting Ingram's then boss Drury on a far larger scale.

When he was interviewed, Ingram implicated Drury, his boss on the Flying Squad, and probably Moody and Virgo, for his close association with Humphreys. Steventon quotes from Ingram's statement, saying that it possibly has some justification. Ingram: 'Like other junior officers I may well have been lulled into a false sense of security as far as this man [Humphreys] is concerned because of his apparent friendliness with officers much senior than myself.' It is a valid point, but it has to be remembered that Ingram was a detective inspector, not a detective constable, and had long service in the Met.

The day after Ingram was interviewed, Ingram voluntarily resigned, and this raised Steventon's eyebrows. Steventon:

> He then had 19 years' service and his sudden decision to abandon a successful career at a stage when he had no pension entitlement was an unusual and extreme step to take. It must give rise to the suggestion that in spite of his protestations of innocence he has some cause for concern over the disclosure of his dealings with Humphreys.

Elsewhere in the report, it is recorded that after his resignation Ingram went to work for the businessman.

★ ★ ★

Finally, to ex-Det. Inspector Ingram's former boss, our old friend, the future blanket-wearing ex-Commander Kenneth Drury. Deputy Assistant Commissioner Kelland dealt with Humphreys' allegations against Drury, and he submitted a report to Deputy Commissioner

Starritt on 10 April 1975. The beginning of the report reiterates the findings of DAC Sheppard of No. 1 Area Inspectorate, who had carried out the initial investigations into Drury's association with Humphreys in late February/March 1972. This had led to Drury's suspension and resignation on pension. But since Humphreys had been jailed for the attack on Garfath, he had made many more allegations. Humphreys obviously knew that the Met was cleaning out its ranks of dirty coppers, and no doubt had an eye on a shortening of his eight-year sentence.

Kelland points out that Humphreys relied on his 1971 and 1972 diaries, the former seized in the raid by Bland and the latter supplied by Rusty, to refresh his memory of events in those years. These were peak years for Humphreys in terms of profit from pornography. Kelland wrote that 'after extensive enquiry, no entry has been proved to be false, whilst the authenticity of many entries has been established.'

Firstly, 'a professional man', (name redacted), whom Kelland describes as a truthful witness, had been interviewed. The man recalled that Drury had admitted to him that 'his newspaper article [*News of the World*, 21 May 1972] branding Humphreys as an informant was a "pack of lies".' This does seem strange, and as Humphreys had admitted being a police informant in his own statements. Humphreys had lied about the Biggs motive for the Cyprus holiday, but this was to help Drury, and to safeguard his own police protection, of course.

It is not impossible that Humphreys had lied about his informing activities, but this is improbable when Humphreys' character and the whole context are considered, especially as Humphreys himself had admitted it to the journalist Laurie Manifold. Humphreys had never denied being an informant to the police when being questioned, and actively brought it up to highlight his past co-operation with the Met. Humphreys only denied being an informant in the newspapers and undoubtedly when asked, as he could have been in real danger from fellow criminals.

Humphreys had also said that he had tape-recorded a conversation with Drury, and that it still existed. But Humphreys refused to hand it over to Kelland and his team, for the reason that 'it contains matters in addition to the Drury conversation which he considers private.' Kelland thought that 'the tape or tapes are being looked after by an agent of Humphreys.'

Then there is the revelation that Drury and Humphreys had been considering going into business together, as wine importers. This had also been corroborated by the 'professional man' who had told the police that Drury said he had lied about Humphreys being an inform-ant. Further confirmation came from a manager of British & Foreign Wharf Co. Ltd, and Kelland wrote that Drury knew others in the wine trade, whom he hoped to introduce to Humphreys.

> Kelland: Whilst it is almost incredible that a senior police officer should have even contemplated a joint business venture with someone of Humphreys' standing, even on the basis that he could actively participate when he had retired, the facts discovered indicate that Drury was so involved. There was no imminence in Drury's retirement and if his ser-vice had followed the normal course he needed to serve until June 1976 before he had a full thirty years' service or until October 1978, when he reached age limit. Seemingly, the money for this venture, which reached the stage of acquiring premises and making licensing applications, was being put up by Humphreys and it was one way in which Drury's influ-ence was being bought.

That was not the only business venture Drury and Humphreys had discussed. Drury had introduced Humphreys to somebody about the possibility of Humphreys promoting a publication which tracked wanted criminals. This had been confirmed by a detective superin-tendent, name redacted. Kelland: 'The idea of a man of Humphreys' background being the promoter of a publication on the lines of *Police 5* is ridiculous, but he was associating at that time with a TV producer, who it seems was being drawn into this venture.' *Police 5* was the fore-runner to the BBC's *Crimewatch* and was presented by Shaw Taylor, whose famous catchphrase was 'Keep your eyes peeled.' It was produced by ATV in association with Scotland Yard, beginning in 1962, and was broadcast throughout the 1970s.

There was also another TV connection. A 'representative, who is closely associated with Independent TV [ITV] sports programmes' had been interviewed twice about an alleged meeting where Drury and Humphreys had been present. Kelland: 'He is a difficult witness and seems determined not to assist this enquiry. Nevertheless he provides corroboration of the meeting ...'

The proprietor of the S.P.Q.R. restaurant in the West End confirmed that Drury had been Humphreys' guest there on 'a number of occasions'. And the proprietor of the Celebrity Club, Aziz 'John' Mehmet, who was the brother of Selim Mehmet, the proprietor of the Boulogne Restaurant whom Drury had mingled with in Cyprus, also said that Drury had been there with Humphreys on one occasion. The Met files show that Aziz 'John' Mehmet bought the premises at 11–12 Clifford Street, Soho, in December 1969. This became the Celebrity Club. Aziz 'John' Mehmet had bought the site from Paul Raymond, the late entrepreneur. Raymond built a large empire from his Raymond Revuebar striptease venue in Great Windmill Street, Soho, pornographic magazines and massive property portfolio.

Rusty Humphreys had also made some statements, firstly to help interpret her husband's diary entries, but also about Drury.

Kelland: Mrs Humphreys had been consistent in her account throughout lengthy interviews and she tells her story convincingly. Although lacking her husband's accuracy in dates and places her evidence goes some way to confirming his account.

Regarding the Cyprus holiday in January 1972, Rusty said that they had originally intended to take the Drurys to their villa in Ibiza. But Rusty said she had felt she had little in common with Drury's wife, so Cyprus had been chosen instead. Kelland said, 'This is in complete accord with Humphreys' account and is far more creditable than the romanticised story of seeking Biggs.' Kelland concluded that the evidence of Humphreys' and Drury's unsubstantiated claim of paying back Humphreys for the holiday in cash, 'all provided a strong inference that Humphreys' claim to have paid the major part of the cost of this holiday is true'.

Rusty also recalled a number of instances of her husband entertaining Drury, and once witnessed Humphreys giving Drury money. Kelland wrote that Rusty also alleged that she had overheard her husband in 'conversation with Mrs Drury over the necklace he had purchased on the occasion of the Flying Squad Annual Dinner … but [this] may not have taken place in Drury's hearing'. Kelland concluded that the evidence of a variety of witnesses proved that Humphreys had been entertaining Drury 'on a lavish scale'. But, apart from Rusty Humphreys' evidence, there was no corroboration of Drury receiving cash or gifts. Humphreys had alleged that he had given Drury several sums of £50 as 'a drink', for a while paid him a weekly retainer of £100, as well as jewellery and other gifts.

It has long been reported by many sources that Humphreys had bought Drury a rowing machine, to work off some of the weight that Drury had gained on his already overweight frame from the fine-dining to which Humphreys had regularly treated him. Kelland had investigated this too. It can now be revealed for the first time that the rowing machine was delivered to Drury at New Scotland Yard, to the Flying Squad office on the fourth floor. A detective inspector, name redacted, had confirmed this.

Humphreys also made the allegation that he had paid Drury £1,000 'as a reward for taking steps to ensure that a plot "to fix him up" [i.e. to secure his arrest by 'planted' evidence] was abandoned'. Of course, it was Bernie Silver who Drury had to calm things over with for Humphreys, as Humphreys had had an affair with Silver's girlfriend Dominique Ferguson which had enraged Silver. In Kelland's report, there is another mention of 'the professional man' who had given a statement to Kelland's team. This man had confirmed that the form that Silver's plot would likely have taken was 'firearms or gelignite being placed in Humphreys' car'. In fact, this is exactly the tactic that Humphreys himself had unsuccessfully used against the Soho club owner Murray Goldstein, as detailed earlier. Kelland stated, 'Obviously Humphreys genuinely believed that such a plot was being hatched by Silver …'

It can also be revealed that two police officers, a detective chief superintendent and an ex-detective superintendent (names redacted) were also 'allegedly concerned' in this plot. Both had been interviewed, and 'denied being party to any such conspiracy'.

Also, a man (name redacted) who had a 'violent dislike and distrust' of Humphreys, recalled 'being required to see Deputy Assistant Commissioner Richard Chitty (since retired) who told him he had heard of such a plot and warned (same name redacted) to have no part in it'. Chitty had of course been Drury's immediate superior officer, and it may be remembered that it was Chitty who told Drury of his suspension in March 1972. The plot against Humphreys had also been confirmed by a 54-year-old property negotiator, an associate of Silver's.

Also regarding Silver, a reference is made to his girlfriend Dominique Ferguson making a complaint to police of Silver assaulting her, shortly after her fling with Humphreys. This is already known, but Kelland's report tells us that when Silver was arrested for assault on a warrant, the ex-detective chief inspector (name redacted) who dealt with the case had recently made a complaint of his own. The ex-detective chief inspector complained, 'through his common-law wife and an MP, that he was ordered not to pursue Silver's prosecution too rigorously. The officers named by him are not connected with this enquiry.' Kelland also states that this same ex-detective chief inspector was then serving a five-year prison term for blackmail and other offences, and that he had been sentenced in December 1973. It also emerges that in Humphreys' 1971 diary, the entry for 13 July read 'Kendal' and a telephone number in Gloucestershire. Kelland reported that Drury had taken some annual leave in Gloucestershire at that time, and that 'Kendal is a pseudonym Humphreys occasionally used for Drury.' Could this pseudonym have been inspired by the late BBC newsreader Kenneth Kendall, who shared a first name with Drury, and was a household name in the 1970s?

Humphreys also made allegations that Drury had admitted taking money from the police funds earmarked for police informants. There is a reference here to the Luton Post Office Murder, and Humphreys' claim here rings true as we know that Drury took a large share of the reward money as part of his damning corruption in that case. So Drury skimming money from informant funds also is only too believable. On Humphreys' allegations, Kelland said: 'He claims that Drury told him that he had 10 per cent of anything his officers drew from the Informants Reward Fund and a further 10 per cent was paid to DAC Chitty.' It should be pointed out here that there is no evidence of Chitty ever being proven guilty of this allegation, or even prosecuted for this offence.

On the Luton Post Office Murder, Kelland said, 'An enquiry is currently being conducted by A10 officers on behalf of the Director of Public Prosecutions respecting allegations that Drury had a half share in a £2,000 reward he paid to a man who gave information leading to the arrest of persons for the murder of a sub-postmaster.'

That man was of course Alf Mathews and in fact Drury took more than just Mathews' share of the reward for the fit-up, as detailed in Chapter Two. The late Sir Ludovic Kennedy never knew that the Met Police was internally investigating Drury's financial arrangements in the Luton Post Office Murder. This was over four years before Kennedy published his book *Wicked Beyond Belief*, which finally got the innocent Cooper and McMahon released from prison.

This makes it even more questionable why Drury was never prosecuted and punished for his corruption in that case, which was of a different depth of venality to his Soho connections, as it ruined lives. A10 may not have found cast-iron proof for the Director of Public Prosecutions. The matter would not be mentioned at Drury's trial. But there are still many questions to be answered as to why Drury escaped punishment when the Home Secretary was moved to release the men. This may also explain why their unsafe convictions were not quashed until 31 July 2003.

Humphreys also detailed how he and Silver dealt with bent coppers. According to Kelland:

> Silver dealt with the senior officers such as ex-Commander Virgo and ex-Det. Chief Supt Alfred Moody and those who had a direct responsibility for enforcing the Obscene Publications Act, whilst he [Humphreys] concerned himself with cultivating the head of the Flying Squad and certain of his officers. Seemingly, middle rank officers from any sphere of police activity whom they thought could be bought or influenced were

fair game to be cultivated by either one or both of these devious and unscrupulous characters.

Kelland concluded that Drury's acceptance of lavish entertainment from Humphreys 'paved the way for other officers, some directly under his command, to accept the largesse being distributed by a man rich from the proceeds of an illegal pornography business'. The allegations against ex-Det. Inspector Alistair Ingram were repeated here. Also, an ex-detective superintendent was allegedly 'given £300 by Humphreys when he was short in order to complete the purchase of his house, and many others became indebted to Humphreys for his generous entertainment'.

Kelland wrote that all of these officers, like Drury, excused their behaviour by saying that they were cultivating Humphreys as an informant:

> Informants come in many guises, but apart from the unlikelihood of working at the same period of time for so many officers ranging in rank from Commander to Det. Sergeant they are not likely to be very successful if they make such a blatant display of their friendship with police, as was the case with both Humphreys and Silver.

Elsewhere in the report, Kelland also clarified his opinion about the informant defence: 'I feel obliged to comment that useful informants are jealously guarded by the officers who cultivate them.' Therefore, it was unlikely that so many police officers would have been happy to share Humphreys.

Drury had been interviewed about Humphreys' new allegations by Kelland's deputy on the inquiry, Commander Ronald Steventon. Drury's solicitor was also present.

> Kelland: Drury declined to reply to almost every question, beyond admitting that he had been in charge of C8 [Flying Squad] during the relevant period and that an entry in Humphreys' diary showing his annual leave telephone number was in his own handwriting. The allegation that Humphreys had been paying him a weekly sum of £100, evoked the response of 'rubbish' and the allegation that during the period of their

association Humphreys had given him a total of £5,000 in cash and had spent a similar sum on entertaining him, led to a reply of 'That is quite untrue.' The interview was under caution and Drury was entitled to exercise his right of silence but it does nothing to refute Humphreys' allegations as they now stand and it is complete contrast to the verbosity he displayed when interviewed during Mr Sheppard's enquiry.

This of course refers to DAC Sheppard's inquiry of late February–March 1972 into the Cyprus holiday.

★ ★ ★

The Dirty Squad would face two trials, consisting of corrupt officers arrested on 28 February 1976, the same day as Drury, and others who had been implicated by the further enquiries of Kelland's team. It was looking dirty with a capital 'D'. Commissioner Mark's restructuring and the crusade against corruption by A10 and No.4 Area Inspectorate would also see many suspensions, and a very large number of resignations and early retirements. During Mark's tenure from 1972–77, no less than 478 police officers retired early, and fifty officers were prosecuted. Mark had taken on the old guard and the highest ranks of the CID, and won. This had been necessary because the systematic corruption had grown within the CID and been allowed to fester there.

The first Dirty Squad trial began on 8 November 1976 at the No.1 Court of the Old Bailey. The Dirty Squad officers in the dock were former Det. Chief Inspector George Fenwick, Det. Inspector Charles O'Hanlon, a detective inspector who was cleared in court so will be unnamed here, Det. Inspector Cyril Jones, Det. Sgt Peter Fisher and Det. Constable Michael Chamberlain. The charge was 'conspiring together and with others to accept money and other considerations from persons trading in pornography between July 1964 and October 1973'. The six were accused of accepting £4,680 in bribes.

The judge was Mr Justice William Mars-Jones, the father of the writer Adam Mars-Jones. Mars-Jones was 61 at the time, and had been a High Court Judge since 1969. In 1964, he had overseen the Home Office inquiry into allegations of corruption in the Metropolitan Police, which had largely been spurred by the arrest of Det. Sgt 'Tanky' Challenor at West End Central. Then in 1966, he prosecuted at the infamous Moors Murders trial of Ian Brady and Myra Hindley, for the sadistic torture and murder of five children in Manchester. Much later in his career, in 1982, he would award a large amount in damages to a Jamaican couple, David and Lucille White, for what Mars-Jones described as a 'brutal, savage and sustained variety of assaults' carried out by the Metropolitan Police when they raided the Stoke Newington home of the couple. Mars-Jones also accused the police of trying to cover up these violent assaults for five years. Mars-Jones died in January 1999.

Seventeen pornographers appeared to give evidence about the allegations of corruption made against the Dirty Squad officers. But Jimmy Humphreys refused, mainly because O'Hanlon was his friend. One of the most colourful moments was when one of the three former members of the Dirty Squad that Kelland's team had assembled for the prosecution gave his evidence. This former detective inspector told how Det. Chief Inspector Fenwick, who had taken over the Dirty Squad after Moody was transferred, had enmeshed him in corruption. This officer said that when they were new to the Dirty Squad, Fenwick would put money (£20) in their pockets at the end of the week. The officer had protested about this, but Fenwick had ignored his pleas. As the officer left that evening with the money, Fenwick had said, 'Handsome, don't panic.' A detective sergeant explained why he could not go to a senior officer by saying, 'I was under the opinion that they were getting the same amount, or other sums of money, that I was getting.'

At the end of the trial, Mr Justice Mars-Jones said, 'Thank goodness the Obscene Publications Squad has gone. I fear the damage you have done may be with us for a long time.' Fenwick received ten years in prison, Jones, Chamberlain and Fisher got eight years, and O'Hanlon seven years. A detective inspector was acquitted on all counts, but he was ordered to pay £2,000 costs.

This was just the warm-up for the second trial, in March 1977. Ex-Commander Harold 'Wally' Virgo, ex-Det. Chief Supt Alfred 'Wicked Bill' Moody, Det. Inspector Leslie Alton, ex-Det. Inspector

Rodney Tilley, Det. Sgt David Hamer and ex-Det. Constable Peter Brown entered the same court, again presided over by Mars-Jones. There were more than thirty pornographers giving evidence this time, including Humphreys, who recalled his 1969 negotiations with Virgo and Moody over his porn licence. It was obvious that Virgo and Moody would attract most flak from the prosecution, as they had committed the most corruption by far. The corruption being prosecuted had taken place between 1964 and 1972. The enormous sum of £87,485 was the total for the twenty-seven counts of bribery and corruption. This was just what had been uncovered.

It was alleged that Moody had accepted the biggest single payment or bribe, £14,000 from pornographer John 'Eric' Mason, aka God, who had paid that sum to have a charge lifted against his manager. This was £4,000 more than Humphreys had paid Moody for his license. The chief prosecuting counsel said in his opening statement that Virgo alone had received £60,000 in illegal payments from pornographers. But it could only be proved that Virgo and Moody combined had received £53,000 in sixteen months, which is almost definitely a conservative estimate.

The harmless-looking Virgo had smoothed things over at a higher level, as he had been of course Head of Central Office and overseer of the elite squads. An example of this is when he had got Det. Chief Supt Fred Lambert, an honest policeman, removed from the *Times* Inquiry. Then Moody had magically arrived on the investigation to hamper Frank Williamson. It came out at the trial that Virgo had first met Bernie Silver in 1965, when he was investigating the murder of the boxer Freddie Mills. The former champion had been found shot dead in his car outside his nightclub, Freddie Mill's Nitespot, in Goslett Yard, just off Charing Cross Road, within shouting distance of Soho. Virgo also maintained that when the name 'Wally', his nickname, appeared in Humphreys' diaries, it didn't refer to him. Virgo said that Humphreys 'hated' him.

Moody was more operational, setting up and negotiating licenses and payments, when not swanning around swinging London in his gleaming Lancia, courtesy of Humphreys. Mr Justice Mars-Jones described this corruption as 'on a scale which beggars description'. Moody was revealed as intimidating to younger, more junior officers, sarcastic and bullying. Moody even asked for a 'transfer fee' of £100 if an officer wanted out of the Dirty Squad, it was alleged. One detective constable thought that Moody was insane. But 'Wicked Bill' wouldn't ride again.

Virgo, aged 58, and Moody, aged 51, received twelve years in prison, Virgo being ordered to pay £15,000 costs, Moody £10,000. Alton got ten years, Brown seven years, Hamer four years and Tilley three years.

But ex-Commander Virgo would have his conviction quashed in August 1978 by the Court of Appeal. The reason given was that Mr Justice Mars-Jones had not directed the jury properly, on the corroboration of the evidence Humphreys had given against Virgo. It was a technicality, and that only, as Virgo was undoubtedly extremely corrupt.

The newspapers were of course having a field day, and had been since the arrests. Now it was the turn of the Flying Squad.

★ ★ ★

No. 1 Court, the Old Bailey, 7 July 1977

Some streets of London were still buzzing with the street parties, remnants of bunting and festivities of the Silver Jubilee, marking twenty-five years of the reign of Queen Elizabeth II the previous month. Other streets reverberated with the anarchic sound of 'God Save the Queen' by the Sex Pistols, which had apathetic young punks pogoing. The former head of the Flying Squad and one of his ex-officers were facing a very different kind of music.

Here he is, ex-Commander Kenneth Drury, former friend and benefactor of Jimmy Humphreys, manipulative framer of the innocent Patrick Murphy, David Cooper and Michael McMahon for the Luton Post Office Murder, the latter two now over seven years into their life sentences. He is 16 stone, and perhaps the most corrupt ex-policeman in the world pound for pound, and act for act, at this moment. Wiping his brow, he affects nonchalance, but the sweat is giving Ken away. No more Talk of the Town, holidays in the sun, the guv'nor, we're the Sweeney, son, the Heavy Mob, no more. No more gateau where he's going, nor fine wines. Just to think that Ken Drury and Jimmy Humphreys might even have imported wines of their own, and had their own label.

Next to Drury, now aged 56, the prematurely grey ex-Det. Inspector Alistair Ingram, aged 43, stands waiting before Mr Justice Pain. They had heard the prosecution counsel refer to their alleged relationship with Humphreys as 'indebting themselves to this tycoon, who was putting himself outside the law'. Prosecution counsel also stated that the £5,000 in cash and £5,000 in hospitality given to Drury was so that Humphreys 'could have a friend in the police who could assist him in time of trouble'. It was also put to the court that Drury was the principal defendant, Ingram 'a much lesser figure'.

★ ★ ★

The trial had begun on 14 June 1977, over three weeks earlier. The court had heard early in proceedings that another suspended detective inspector of the Flying Squad, aged 37, who had stood beside Drury and Ingram, owed his position there mainly due to Drury. It was said that the detective inspector had allegedly benefitted from Humphreys' bribes to please Drury. This officer had been arraigned on two charges of corruption, and after a submission by his counsel, Brian Appleby QC, he was acquitted. The officer said after that he would 'certainly be looking outside the police force for my future career.' He added 'I have been suspended from duty since December 31, 1973, the longest ever in the Metropolitan Police. I have always protested my innocence.'

A 15 July 1977 report in the Met files, addressed to Deputy Assistant Commissioner Kelland, states, 'Humphreys, in evidence, did not come up to proof in relation to his association with [the officer], this resulted in the judge directing he be acquitted of the charges.' That judge was Mr Justice Peter Pain, who had stood unsuccessfully for election as an MP for Farnham, Surrey, in 1937, representing the Labour Party, and this reflected Pain's left-wing political views. After becoming a lawyer, he had been made a QC in 1965, and in the 1960s until 1975, he specialised in labour law, representing industrial injury victims and trade unions. In 1975, Pain became a High Court Judge, and that's how he was faced with the three Flying Squad officers, two resigned and one suspended, in 1977. Pain died in January 2003.

David Tudor-Price, Senior Treasury Counsel, appeared for the Prosecution, with Michael Nelligan as his junior counsel. Drury was represented by the German-born and former youthful alien internee George Shindler QC. 'Mad' Frankie Fraser once rejected him as his defence brief, as Shindler had prosecuted one of Fraser's criminal associates. Victor Durand QC represented Ingram. Durand had represented Jimmy Nash, allegedly the straightest of the gangland Nash brothers, alongside Joey Pyle, at the Pen Club trial in 1960, for the killing of Selwyn Cooney, as detailed earlier. Nash was acquitted of murder, but got five years for grievous bodily harm.

Of course both Drury and Ingram pleaded not guilty. One of the most memorable moments of the trial occurred when Rusty Humphreys, who the *Sun* described as 'a redheaded ex-stripper', gave evidence against Drury. After a rigorous cross-examination by George Shindler QC, Rusty told the court:

> If you have any doubts you can give me a truth drug. Give Mr Drury a
> truth drug. I do not really want to give evidence against this man, but it
> is my duty and I am doing it. I do not like being called a liar.'

Incidentally, the Met files show that Ingram had written to the police about Humphreys, and that this letter was forwarded to the Home Secretary on 9 March 1977. Unfortunately, the contents of this letter were not disclosed under Freedom of Information. A letter from the Home Office to the Met in the files shows that Humphreys was manoeuvring behind the scenes through his solicitor to have his conviction for the Garfath assault looked into again too. There is no doubt that a key motivation for Humphreys giving evidence at the second Dirty Squad and the Flying Squad trials was to earn himself some bargaining power for remission.

In the end, Ingram, whom one newspaper described as Drury's 'right-hand man', went down for accepting the £900 Singer Vogue Estate car, a £50 'drink', and free labour for the bathroom suite fitting at his home from Humphreys. He was cleared of three charges of accepting entertainment. Ingram received four years in prison.

Drury, who during the trial seemed to revel in his underworld connections, was audacious at times, tough and uncompromising. For those who didn't know the true extent of his corruption and venality, he was almost a larger-than-life maverick, John Thaw's Det. Inspector Regan of *The Sweeney* TV show made flesh, a man's man, ex-leader of the Heavy Mob. Convicted of accepting a £60 pair of sovereign cufflinks, but acquitted of accepting the £60 necklace for his wife Joan, it all seemed almost decadently naughty. But when all of his corruption in relation to Humphreys, the cash, hospitality and holiday were taken into account, Drury got eight years. The next day, it would be reported that Drury's wife Joan was in shock and close to a nervous breakdown. In 1978, Drury's eight years would be reduced to five years by the Court of Appeal, as it had not been found that Drury had influenced or cajoled other officers into corruption.

There was no mention of A10's investigation of Drury's receiving part of the Luton Post Office Murder reward money. It would be another three years and eleven days until David Cooper and Michael McMahon were released, and another thirty-six years before their convictions were posthumously quashed. But then we already know the full horror of Drury's corruption in that case, and the tragic consequences of his actions.

But Mr Justice Pain said in his closing speech that both Drury and Ingram were 'a serious threat to law and order' because of their corruption.

> Mr Justice Pain: 'It is difficult for those of us who sit at these courts to expect juries to convict on police evidence when they read in the newspapers of some of the matters for which policemen have been convicted … When there is a lack of leadership at the top, it clearly affects the work of junior officers.'

He also stated that both Drury and Ingram would 'go to jail in fear'. Victor Durand QC had protested that both men would be in danger from fellow prisoners hostile to the police. If he had known and been prosecuting rather than defending, Durand might have added that

Drury would be in particular danger if he ever came across the innocent he had fitted up in prison, or those associated with them.

The judge gave credit to Laurie Manifold and the *Sunday People*, saying, 'We owe a debt to the press for exposing the Cyprus holiday.' This was of course the lever that opened the stench-laden box of corruption, and it was Drury's arrogance and feelings of being all-powerful which took it further. By naming Humphreys as a grass in the multi-million-selling *News of the World*, Drury provoked a reaction and the unravelling of the tarnished tapestry of corruption began. The Metropolitan Police were also commended by Pain, specifically DAC Kelland's team of No.4 Inspectorate and A10 officers. 'I realise that the work of investigating fellow officers, necessary though it is, must be singularly distasteful and I will be glad if you will convey the thanks of the court ...'

But it was just one sentence spoken by Mr Justice Pain with gravity and a theatrical pause midway through that would have hurt the previously all-powerful ex-Head of the Flying Squad most of all. Just before the red-faced and sweating Drury was led to the cells below the Old Bailey, Pain said, 'The bigger you are ... the harder you fall.'

Drury would also be stripped of his pension, and officially erased from the Flying Squad headquarters, when his photograph was taken down from outside the Commander's office soon after. But perhaps the last word on these corrupt officers should go here to the then Home Secretary, whose letter of 19 October 1978 is in the Met files:

I, the Rt. Hon. Merlyn Rees, MP, one of her Majesty's Principal Secretaries of State, do in pursuance of Clause 13 of the Royal warrant of 14 June 1951, hereby order that the Police Long Service and Good Conduct Medals awarded to Kenneth Ronald Drury, Alfred William Moody and Leslie Frank Alton, formerly of the Metropolitan Police, be forfeited; and that their names be deleted from the record of those to whom the Medal has been awarded.

7

CRAWLING FROM THE ABYSS

JIMMY HUMPHREYS WAS released from Maidstone Prison in mid July 1977, just a week after his former friends Drury and Ingram of the Flying Squad went down. Humphreys had been in solitary confinement towards the end of his sentence, after being attacked by a fellow prisoner who accused him of being a 'grass'. So whilst Drury had gone to prison largely through Humphreys' allegations, Drury's 21 May 1972 *Sunday People* insinuations that Humphreys was a police informer had severely compromised Jimmy's status in the underworld. Amongst criminals, child killers, paedophiles and grasses have always been *persona non grata*.

Rusty Humphreys told the newspapers that her husband was first going to finish 'the tough, Mickey Spillane-type novel' he had begun penning in prison. She also said, 'He has made plans for the future, and he's going to make a success of his life.' Humphreys, now 47, had served three years and eight months of his eight year sentence for wounding Garfath. The Home Office confirmed that his early release was 'in recognition of the help he had given the police in the prosecution and conviction of thirteen former detectives on corruption charges'.

But Jimmy wasn't finished yet. Four days after his release, he told the *Sunday People*, the newspaper which had exposed his holiday with Drury five and a half years earlier, that there were nine allegedly corrupt detectives still in the Metropolitan Police. Humphreys said that he had paid bribes to these members of the CID, and that he had informed the police about them. But he alleged that the Met had failed to take action against those officers. The article reported that Humphreys had made a full statement of his allegations to his solicitor, and that this would be passed on to the Home Secretary 'on condition that the police hand over their own file on Mr Humphreys'. Humphreys was never given his file, and its contents were not divulged until the publication of this book. This may explain why there was no publicised inquiry into these allegations, although as mentioned earlier, there was a very sharp increase in early police retirements and resignations during 1972–77.

The main focus of these new allegations against the nine detectives was that they had taken a cut of insurance money which should have gone to informers. This seems suspiciously like what Drury had told him about taking 10 per cent of the police informant fund. We know that Drury took a large cut of the reward money on the Luton Post Office Murder case. Drury had also apparently said that at least one other senior officer had taken such a cut of the informant fund. But just how widespread had it been: was it an automatic 'perk'? We will never know for sure. Humphreys also alleged that he knew the name of a detective who was paid to smuggle drugs through Heathrow airport, and that he would name a former Scotland Yard officer who ran a pub where a bribery and corruption racket was based. Humphreys claimed too that in his heyday he had made £2,000 a week from pornography, but that a few hundred of that was paid out in police bribes weekly.

Humphreys even made the point that some honest and hard-working officers had never received promotion because they had upset criminals who were paying bribes to senior officers in return for immunity from prosecution. This was undoubtedly true. It was a symptom of men such as Humphreys and Silver paying men such as Drury, Moody and Virgo, and well as others, large amounts in kickbacks and 'drinks'.

The morale within the CID at New Scotland Yard and the Metropolitan Police as a whole had of course taken a severe knock. The massive necessary restructuring brought about by Commissioner Sir Robert Mark had been unsettling for the old guard of detectives, especially at senior levels. But then this was where the corruption had been allowed to flourish, and the cause for the difficulties Mark had faced. There is no doubt that those five years at the helm had taken a toll on Mark. However, Mark had achieved his aim of rooting out the most corrupt. The slew of resignations and retirements added to the shakeup, although some were likely caused by an inability to work within and accept the new CID order.

Sir David McNee succeeded Mark as Commissioner of the Met on 13 March 1977. McNee was a Glaswegian who had served on Glasgow's own Flying Squad in his career, before becoming Chief Constable of Strathclyde Police. In his memoirs, McNee wrote that when he took over as Commissioner, 'the force was disconcerted and unsettled.' McNee explained that one of the reasons for this was 'the aftermath of extensive investigations into corruption, particularly within the CID'.

What was it like for a new police officer starting a career in the Metropolitan Police in the mid to late 1970s? This author interviewed former Det. Inspector Andrew Gorzynski, who joined the Met in 1976, and went on to work in vice in Stoke Newington, northeast London. Gorzynski said, 'When I joined in 1976, the first thing I heard was that morale was at rock bottom.' This is little wonder. After all the publicity given to the corruption in the Met, from the *Times* Inquiry in 1969, the Drug Squad scandal of 1972, the Flying Squad saga 1972–77, and the Dirty Squad's exposure 1976–77, the Met's public image was very tarnished. It must have been felt very keenly within the ranks.

Gorzynski remembers a very male-dominated environment, with only one female on his relief. It was also a time of turbulence: the murder of Blair Peach, the teacher killed in an anti-racism protest in April 1979 (a Met report released in 2010 showed that Peach's death was most likely caused by elite riot police officers); the problems with the fascist National Front and football hooliganism, sometimes intertwined; social unrest, especially the Brixton riots of 1981; and other protests connected to the Unions, mainly marches. Jim Callaghan would be succeeded by Margaret Thatcher as Prime Minister in 1979 and the political and social landscape of Britain was changing. At this time, Gorzynski was a Police Constable in uniform. How did the uniform and CID branches think of each other? According to Gorzynski:

The uniform branch is very different from CID. I was in uniform, so I was probably slightly biased. Uniform don't like CID, CID don't like the Diplomatic Protection Branch. Everybody's got it better than somebody else. The CID could get the overtime. Specialist squads like the Flying Squad would be seen as no more than 'they've got it easy' … even the CID weren't looked up to, as they were seen as encroaching on our patch. There was also a lot of rivalry between Special Branch and MI5.

On the calibre of officers in the Flying Squad, Gorzynski said:

In all specialist squads, they are all very good, skilled officers … but … sometimes when you move into specialist fields, some people start to feel they are working outside the organisation, sometimes that can make you very specialised, very narrow. Then when you come back to reality, you have to comply with the rules and regulations of the rest of the organisation.

This is undoubtedly the self-empowering and independent feeling that Drury's Flying Squad and Moody and Fenwick's Dirty Squad felt. This free rein and lack of scrutiny allowed them to think that they were working outside of the Met. Due to that autonomy, they could do what they wanted and get away with it.

This certainly must have added to the shock for men such as Drury and Moody when they were suspended, arrested and imprisoned. Until then they had been seemingly omnipotent, in their own minds and in their own squad-world. This was one of the reasons that Mark brought in rotation between CID and uniform at regular intervals, to stop this build-up of power. This would have surely hindered Drury, Moody and Virgo in their corruption, stopping them from building up such deep-rooted corrupt networks. But those three were already very powerful, high-ranking officers anyway, of course. It also has to be remembered that Drury's worst corruption was committed in the Murder Squad, prior to becoming Head of the Flying Squad. However, if Mark's rotation system had come in during the 1950s, these officers may have been stymied in their rise. On Commissioner Mark, Gorzynski said, 'He was well respected. The police constables thought he was great.'

In the 1970s the way to get ahead in the Met was through arrests, and the real route to advancement was in the CID, but there were politics involved.

> Gorzynski: When I first started, there was a big emphasis on numbers – if you wanted to go into the CID, you needed arrests. The way to CID rank was through CID. In the 1970s/1980s, if you wanted to get on in the CID, it was very much who you knew … Friday afternoon drink, which probably started at about 11 o'clock!

Gorzynski also remembered policing before the Police and Criminal Evidence Act of 1984 (PACE), which regulated police powers, as detailed in the Introduction:

> All the way up to 1984, when you interviewed someone, there was no CCTV, no taping, statements from witnesses were relied on. When you made an arrest, nobody else was in the custody area … These days the Custody Sergeant can't be bullied.

Pre-PACE was a police world in which corruption thrived systemically. Gorzynski also pointed out that pre-PACE police officers were more vulnerable too, as criminals could make untrue allegations against them.

Gorzynski never witnessed any corruption himself, but did know officers who had gone to prison, one for importing drugs. Gorzynski always played by the book himself, keeping abreast of new legislation: 'I didn't want to be caught out.' On accepting gifts or hospitality, he said: 'I would accept a coffee, but never any money or a meal even. You've got to be careful.' Regarding Ex-Commander Drury, he commented: 'He must have been so confident that he was never going to get a knock on the door. He must have dominated everything around him.' On the mentality of intimidation of subordinate officers, evidence of which was given against ex-Det. Chief Supt Moody at his trial, Gorzynski summed up the way of thinking: 'I dominate you. I control your career.'

The racially motivated murder of the black teenager Stephen Lawrence in 1993 would have a huge impact on the Met throughout the 1990s. Twenty years later, in 2013, allegations surfaced that officers of the Met had covertly been ordered to dig some dirt to discredit the Lawrence family in the nineties, who had been vociferous in campaigning for justice for Stephen, and the way that his murder had been investigated. Gorzynski remembered the 1990s shake-up:

> When I look back at the investigation into Stephen Lawrence – I wasn't involved in it so I'm not making observations about the investigation – there was huge fallout when the Met was found to be institutionally racist, there were meetings where every rank and file had to attend. To learn, to move forward, to see it as a chance to improve; massive resources thrown at it, not just every rank, but civil staff, etc.

Gorzynski stressed that the Met was much more professional and inclusive now than it was when he joined in 1976. 'The Met has moved forward so much because of its problems in the past.' But Gorzynski also remembered a major inquiry which took place early in his police career, into alleged police corruption, the year after members of the Flying Squad and Dirty Squad went down. But it wasn't on the scale of the Lawrence Inquiry in the 1990s.

> As a PC in the late 1970s, we spoke about [Operation] Countryman in the canteen. I knew it as a name, but I didn't really understand what Countryman was. It didn't filter down to the ordinary, the level I was at. Occasionally people would mention Countryman … People didn't talk about it because it maybe didn't affect them.

★ ★ ★

The allegations which led to Operation Countryman in 1978 had come from inside the Metropolitan Police, in fact from the Flying Squad. By now, Drury's successor, Commander Locke, had been replaced by Commander Don Neesham as Head of the Flying Squad. Neesham was a recipient of the Queen's Police Medal, and had previously served under Jack Slipper on the Flying Squad. Neesham now passed on information he had that there was corruption in the City of London Police. In August 1978, the Home Secretary Merlyn Rees ordered an external investigation to be carried out by Assistant Chief Constable Leonard Burt of Dorset Police, overseen by Burt's Chief Constable, Arthur Hambleton. As Dorset is a rural county in the southwest of England, the name 'Countryman' was chosen. Unfortunately, metropolitan snobbery and feelings of being elite led to the team carrying out the operation being given the nickname 'The Swedey' within some parts of the CID. This was a play on the Sweeney and the vegetable grown in rural areas. This derogatory term became widely used especially after the allegations of corruption came back to haunt the Flying Squad itself.

Various books written by ex-Met police officers have given the impression that Leonard Burt, who would retire as Assistant Chief Constable of Dorset in December 1984, was unsophisticated and not up to the Countryman job. In fact, Burt had had a long and distinguished career, including helping bring in the Portland Spy Ring in 1961, for which he had been commended by the Lord Chief Justice for his efforts.

Operation Countryman would not be wrapped up until 1982, and would cost, at various estimates, between £2 million and £3 million. It was controversial, and that controversy still remains today. Countryman would also involve supergrasses giving evidence against police officers of both the City of London Police, which had its own Commissioner and was independent, and the Metropolitan Police. Peter Marshall, the Commissioner of the City of London Police had asked the Chief Inspector of Constabulary to investigate his force. This request had in turn been kicked upstairs to the Home Secretary, who authorised it, as it would be publicly funded. But it was the Deputy Commissioner of the Metropolitan Police, Patrick Kavanagh, who asked that connected allegations against Met officers be included in Countryman's remit.

Neesham's initial allegation was that City of London Police officers had corrupt links to armed robbers. This was centred on three major crimes: a payroll robbery at the offices of the *Daily Express* in 1976 which netted £175,000; a robbery outside the headquarters of Williams & Glyn's Bank in London in 1977, in which £225,000 was stolen; and most seriously, a £200,000 robbery at the offices of the *Daily Mirror* in

1978, during which a security guard named Antonio Castro, aged 38, was shot dead.

Working out of Camberwell Police Station in south London, Burt and his team began its task. But after Burt complained that somebody had tried to 'interfere' with the Countryman team's paperwork, the operation's base moved to Godalming Police Station, in Surrey. The implication was that somebody from inside the City of London or Metropolitan Police forces had caused this interference, and so it was thought prudent to move the inquiry out of London. In his 1983 memoirs, ex-Met Commissioner Sir David McNee scoffed at how logistically impractical this was, as it had meant so much more travel for the Countryman team to do its job.

But it has to be said that the tone of almost everything McNee wrote about the operation was anti-Countryman. McNee was at the very pinnacle of the Met, and one can see how the nickname 'The Swedey' stuck. McNee said, 'Burt encouraged the team to see themselves as being some general anti-corruption squad dedicated to cleaning up the Metropolitan Police.' The cynicism is there between the lines, the rural outsiders investigating *us*, the biggest police force in the country, covering London, the capital, the centre of all. But it would go much further than snide nicknames and condescension. The Operation Countryman team would be confronted with widespread obstruction from both senior and lower police ranks.

This is obviously why Burt instructed his team not to inform Commissioner McNee or Deputy Commissioner Kavanagh of any evidence gathered implicating Metropolitan Police Officers in corruption. This was after McNee said that the Met would be pleased to take responsibility for 'any complaints and information unrelated to the inquiry which they cared to pass to us'. The trust just wasn't there. The implication for the Countryman team was presumably that the Met wanted to investigate claims of improper conduct made against its own officers. Burt's Countryman team was being encouraged to concentrate on the initial allegations made by Neesham, against the City of London Police.

The methods used by Countryman included sending police officers undercover to gather information, an echo of the Ghost Squad of the late 1940s. But unlike the Ghost Squad, the Countryman team were gathering intelligence against police officers rather than criminals. The evidence of at least one 'supergrass' was used, and this obviously discomforted some in the Met. McNee:

> All sorts of tittle-tattle by criminals, by associates of criminals, or by disgruntled complainants was listened to and acted upon. Some of the allegations may have been made in good faith but much animosity towards particular police officers or with hope of obtaining early release from prison or some other benefit.

He had a point, but one has to remember that such information from criminals could expose corrupt police officers. Drury would never have been prosecuted if it were not for Humphreys' allegations.

The allegations being made to Countryman about officers of the Flying Squad were that some were involved in accepting bribes from serious criminals in return for the lessening or dropping of charges and intelligence tip-offs about operations and coming raids. This was obviously very worrying to the Met top brass so soon after Drury and Ingram had so very publicly started eating porridge. The detailed nature of these allegations is still not known, and access to them is denied under Freedom of Information, due to public interest immunity. But it is known that members of the Flying Squad had made complaints within the Met CID that the Countryman team had been approaching their informants for information without their knowledge. Was this purely a professional concern? These new allegations against the Flying Squad must surely have contributed to the coming devolvement of the Flying Squad too.

And were the Met trying to gain control of the investigation into allegations into its own officers, as both Burt and Hambleton would later claim? Or can McNee be believed? That he was only concerned about the length and cost of the inquiry, as the Director of Prosecutions Sir Thomas Hetherington certainly was too. McNee and Hetherington were also critical of the calibre of Burt's Countryman team, especially after the arrest of a City of London police officer, whose prosecution had to be dropped due to the case against him not being strong enough. A meeting did eventually take place between Burt's superior in the Dorset Police, Chief Constable Arthur Hambleton, and Met Deputy Commissioner Patrick Kavanagh. Hambleton had said in a television interview on the *World in Action* political programme that he had been coerced into signing a statement by the Met saying that there had been no obstruction. At the consequent meeting between Hambleton and Kavanagh, Hambleton alleged that Don Neesham, the Head of the Flying Squad, and the supplier of the original corruption allegations, had been less than helpful to the Countryman team.

This was apparently investigated by the Met, according to McNee, but no evidence was found that Neesham had been obstructive, just that he had perhaps been overprotective of his Flying Squad officers. This was because Countryman had been looking into allegations of corruption linked to the Flying Squad too, although McNee doesn't mention this in so many words. But Neesham was to be sidelined anyway. McNee said, 'In order once again to avoid any accusation of obstruction to the Countryman inquiry, it was decided to move Neesham to other duties. When told of this, however, he exercised his right to retire on pension.'

Added to this, not very long after he retired as Chief Constable of Dorset in February 1980, Hambleton made allegations too. Hambleton alleged that Operation Countryman had been purposefully obstructed in carrying out its enquiries by Sir Thomas Hetherington, the Director of Public Prosecutions, and Commissioner McNee. This was a charge which McNee vehemently denied. McNee also said that before he retired, Hambleton had agreed to the Operation Countryman inquiry being completed under the direction of Sir Peter Matthews, Chief Constable of Surrey Police, in which county the team was based. Assistant Chief Constable Leonard Burt would return to Dorset on 1 May 1980. Sir Peter Matthews did take control of Countryman. But what did Sir Peter Matthews do soon after? He passed the investigation of allegations against the Metropolitan Police back to the Met itself, in the form of the Complaint Investigation Bureau (CIB).

This meant that the Met would be investigating itself, precisely what the Chief Inspectorate of Constabulary and the Home Secretary had not wanted in 1978, and why Burt and Hambleton had been drafted in from outside the Met in the first place. Not just that, but Sir Peter Matthews now had Deputy Assistant Commissioner Ronald Steventon, who had been promoted, as his No.2 on Countryman. Steventon had done a thorough job on the A10/No.4 Inspectorate investigation into pornography and corruption under DAC Gilbert Kelland, who was now Assistant Commissioner (CID). But Steventon was a very senior officer in the Met, not an entirely objective outsider.

In the end, eight Metropolitan Police officers investigated by Operation Countryman were brought to trial. All were acquitted. Two of them were subsequently dismissed from the Met through internal disciplinary hearings, and one resigned. The verdicts on the last of the Operation Countryman prosecutions eventually came to the No.1 Court of the Old Bailey on 22 March 1982. This involved four of those eight officers, a detective inspector, a detective sergeant and two detective constables.

They were all accused of corruption, and three of perverting the course of justice, regarding a 1977 armed robbery which netted £18,000. But as just mentioned, they were acquitted on all counts. The detective inspector waved at the jury and said, 'Thank you, thank you,' when the verdict was announced. But in court that day, evidence was given by a man who would allege that the Metropolitan Police had conspired against him. These allegations would be repeated some twenty-eight years later.

John Twomey had been arrested in 1977 for an armed robbery on a branch of the NatWest Bank in the Bayswater Road, west London. A sawn-off shotgun had been found at his home in a search. But Twomey alleged that the firearm had been planted by the police, and that it actually belonged to the father of one of the police officers who had been investigating him. Born in Ireland but brought up in Paddington, west London as well as borstal, Twomey *was* an armed robber. He had carried out his first job in 1971 on a local government building in Westminster in central London, from which £27,000 was officially stolen. Twomey claimed that individual gang cuts had been £2,000 apiece. He had been caught and received five years.

Although Twomey's evidence had not convicted any of the police officers that day, the charges against him for the 1977 NatWest robbery had been dropped due to the allegations of corruption surrounding the case. But soon after leaving court that day in March 1982, he was arrested again for alleged involvement in an armed robbery in 1981. For this, Twomey was later acquitted, and was also awarded substantial damages from the Metropolitan Police.

Fast forward to 2004, when there was a £1.75 million robbery from a warehouse at Heathrow airport, for which Twomey was arrested as the mastermind. There would be four trials for this offence in total, the first stopped as Twomey suffered a serious heart attack, the second and third abandoned due to alleged jury tampering. The fourth trial took place in 2010, which was heard without a jury to avoid tampering, the first serious criminal trial in Britain in which this was done. Twomey was found guilty and sentenced to twenty years and six months. On 13 October 2011, Twomey was denied a Supreme Court appeal. In an interview with the *Guardian*, before his conviction on 31 March 2010, Twomey had said, 'It's quite personal between me and the Metropolitan Police. I feel they are determined to get me.' Twomey's case is a classic example of a jury's dilemma, even if a jury did not convict Twomey in 2010. Do you accept the allegations of a convicted armed robber against police officers, which they had not in the Operation Countryman trials in 1982? Such evidence needs corroboration in court. In the case of the Flying Squad and Dirty Squad officers a few years before, there had been independent corroboration of guilt from other criminals, as well as from within the police itself.

Operation Countryman has always been contentious. Three hundred police officers were investigated in total, belonging to both the City of London and Metropolitan Police forces. Twenty-five of those officers had been facing charges at one point, allegedly including some as high as the rank of divisional commander. Could prosecutions have been achieved if there had not been alleged obstruction from the Metropolitan Police, and if Assistant Chief Constable Burt of the Dorset Police had concluded the inquiry? This will never be known, and until the details of Operation Countryman are fully disclosed, including those allegations made against the Flying Squad, questions and suspicions will remain. What is certain is that coming so soon after the corruption scandals of the Flying Squad and Dirty Squad, the wide media publicity which Countryman attracted did little to help public confidence and morale within the Met CID. But then the fact that there were no convictions as a result of it was fortunate for the Metropolitan Police too.

★ ★ ★

In 1978, Lord Edmund-Davies was assigned to lead an inquiry into police pay by the Home Secretary. It was widely felt that the police were underpaid. But this is of course no mitigation for the large-scale corruption and bribe-taking revealed in the elite squads of the Metropolitan Police during that decade. In Britain, the police are not allowed to strike by law. This has been the law since the formation of the Police Federation in 1919, the same year as the Flying Squad began to taxi to take-off. But dissatisfaction and protest over pay was growing within ranks during the 1970s. And in 1977, when the country was in some social and economic turmoil, effectively fig-leaved by the Silver Jubilee, there was genuine fear that the police could strike. At a time of social unrest and discontent, this was especially thought to be a danger to civil order.

Callaghan's Labour Government had offered a 5 per cent rise in police pay, but inflation was running at an astronomical 15 per cent in 1977. Home Secretary Merlyn Rees received a cold reception at the Police Federation annual conference, and the government raised its offer to a 10 per cent pay-rise. The Police Federation wanted between 78 per cent and 104 per cent, and industrial action was threatened. In October, Merlyn Rees was shouted down when addressing the Metropolitan Police Federation.

But the Police Federation for the whole of Britain did accept a 10 per cent rise, with the added promise of an independent inquiry, and so Lord Edmund-Davies was appointed. Edmund-Davies concluded in his report in 1978 that substantial police pay increases of up to 40 per cent should be awarded, on the condition that the police would never strike.

The government agreed to bring this in over two years, with a 20 per cent increase each year, and when Margaret Thatcher's Conservatives came to power in 1979, it was introduced fully. That year would also see the introduction of a new Force Inspectorate. It was hoped that this would be more effective in identifying police wrongdoing and investigating complaints, wiping away the threat of intimidation by corrupt officers. As we have seen in this book, such intimidation had taken place in elite squads, as well as in uniform, during the 1960s and 1970s.

There was a changing culture of the police in Britain at this time. The fear of police strikes was obviously the main factor in getting government to agree eight times its original offer. But the deep corruption which had come to light in the Met in the 1970s obviously had an influence too. The speech made by John Thaw's character Det. Inspector Jack Regan in *The Sweeney* TV show quoted in the introduction reflected the real feeling within the Met at this time. Ex-Det. Inspector Andrew Gorzynski confirmed to this author that it was a real issue. Better-paid police also meant less temptation to go on the take. But it would likely have made no difference to deeply corrupt officers such as Drury, Moody and Virgo, as the scale of their taking was way beyond salary supplementation.

The year 1978 also saw the devolvement of the Flying Squad. As Dick Kirby points out, 'Eighty per cent of the Squad's workforce had left the Yard.' The duties of the Flying Squad (Central Office No.8 Squad, CO08) were given to the Central Robbery Squad. And in August 1983, a year after Sir David McNee was succeeded as Met Commissioner by Sir Kenneth Newman, this was narrowed further. Inner London armed robberies were assigned to No. 5 Central Robbery Squad, which was made up of Nos 9, 10, 11 and 12 Squads. Operations were no longer based at New Scotland Yard, but at bases in north-east, north, south-east and south-west London. Four senior detectives were still at New Scotland Yard overseeing operations, but most of the work was done at those four branches.

So, the Flying Squad was no more. The name would continue to be used colloquially and still is. This is no great surprise, as it is not just a household name but an international one. It has never been the same again though. Sights such as Drury receiving his rowing machine, gruffly answering his dial-phone with a fag in the other hand, or Flying Squad members reading his postcard from Cyprus on the office notice-board, are long gone.

The irony was that Drury saw himself as a Flying Squad man through and through, its commander, the 'guv'nor'. He repeatedly expressed his loyalty to his men, revelling in the macho bonding of this elite and legendary Metropolitan Police unit. The Flying Squad had of course carried out many brave exploits and successful operations, clearing the streets of heavy-duty criminals, year after year. But as Drury served his prison sentence, word must have got to him about the devolvement of the Flying Squad. Drury surely knew that more than anyone else he was guilty of bringing the Flying Squad to an end, almost sixty years after Det. Superintendent Fred Wensley was given the authority to form the four units which began the Flying Squad experiment in 1919.

If Drury felt no conscience or moral twinge for the depraved way he had behaved in totality, he should have realised his culpability for the Flying Squad's demise. With the exposure of his holiday with Humphreys, and his further blind arrogance in naming Jimmy Humphreys as an informer, Drury not only brought about his own downfall. Drury also provided Commissioner Mark with the lever he needed with which to clean out the CID, and bring down the Flying Squad as Drury knew it.

That corruption had grown over decades, and by the early 1970s, very senior officers such as Drury and Moody were brazenly bent, and those under them, particularly in Moody's case, were often part of that corruption too. Institutionalised corruption grows if unchecked, but it's the culture that feeds it.

CODA

Ex-Commander Kenneth Drury

After serving his reduced sentence, Drury disappeared into obscurity. He died in 1984, at the age of 63. In his will, Drury had asked for his old Flying Squad officers to be bought a drink, and for the London telephone directories to be buried with him, in case he wanted to call any of them up. It's very doubtful that Drury would have called the numbers of Jimmy Humphreys or any of the innocent people he had framed.

Ex-Det. Inspector Alistair Ingram

Ingram reached the age of 80 in January 2014, and lives in Gloucestershire. He was a company director of Stroud Masonic Hall Ltd between the years 2000 and 2010.

Ex-Det. Chief Supt Alfred William Moody

'Wicked Bill' is still alive, but could not be traced. He is in late 80s, and presumably not driving a vintage Lancia, but if you see an elderly man on a mobility scooter that is shinier and better than everybody else's, it could be old Bill.

Ex-Commander Harold 'Wally' Virgo

Virgo died in 1980, after suffering another major heart attack. The late notorious cat burglar Peter Scott, on whom the 1965 film *He Who Rides a Tiger* was based, told the journalist Duncan Campbell that when he saw Virgo after he was convicted (later cleared on a technicality), Wally couldn't look him in the eye.

Jimmy Humphreys

Humphreys never did write that crime novel. Soon after coming out of prison, he and Rusty went to County Limerick, Ireland, and moved from porn to drugs, starting a greyhound breeding company, really just a front for an amphetamine factory. But when the Irish police went to arrest him, Humphreys had characteristically already gone. In 1994, a Dublin police spokesman said that this warrant for Humphreys' arrest would not be pursued any longer, as the prosecution witnesses were not available. Next, Jimmy and Rusty were in Miami, Florida, where Jimmy got seriously ripped off by the big boys after allegedly investing in a mafia drug shipment and it was rumoured that Mexico and Colombia were their next stops. But in the early 1990s, Jimmy and Rusty returned to London, and were soon involved in vice again, this time prostitution. After renting three high-class flats in central London, prostitutes paid rent and other expenses to Jimmy and Rusty: £100-180 a day rent, £30 a day for gas and electricity, £100–200 a week for the printing of 'business' cards to be placed in telephone boxes, and £50 a day for the team of 'card boys' who distributed the cards. The profits made by Jimmy and Rusty were large, by any standards but their own – £100,000 in twenty months between March 1992 and November 1993, when they were arrested. Eight of the call girls gave statements to the police (one had been advertised as 'Nurse Diana' and gave enemas), and Jimmy received twelve months, Rusty eight months in prison at Southwark Crown Court. Jimmy Humphreys died in Hastings, Sussex, in September 2003, aged 73, apparently in negotiations for a film about his life at the time of his death.

Bernie Silver

On his release from prison in 1978, Silver moved to Malta, but was deported soon after, and returned to the West End. He still had stakes in several establishments in Soho, but with the Syndicate smashed, it was never the same, although the *Sunday People* informed its readers that he was back in town. His wife, Albertine Falzon, a French prostitute – not to be confused with his previously mentioned long-time girlfriend Dominique Ferguson- committed suicide in the late 1970s by jumping from the upper floor of her working premises in Peter Street, Soho.

Frank Mifsud

After the quashing of his conviction and release, 'Big Frank' went back to Switzerland and allegedly lived very comfortably off of his savings deposited in Swiss bank accounts. Other members of the Syndicate are said to have ended up in Switzerland too, but it is unknown if they were fond of a fondue.

BIBLIOGRAPHY

Files

Metropolitan police files requested and access granted through Freedom of Information concerning: Flying Squad: ex-Commander Kenneth Drury, ex-Inspector Alistair Ingram; Obscene Publications Unit: ex-Chief Superintendent Bill Moody; overall commander of squads ex-Commander Wally Virgo; James 'Jimmy' Humphreys, Bernie Silver, Frank Mifsud, and other prominent convicted criminals mentioned in association. Other officers convicted and associates are also named in the files released; those not prosecuted have had their names redacted.

MEPO2/9538, Murder of John Beckley, Clapham Common, 1953 and the
    Conviction of Michael John Davies,
National Archives J 82/4017, Director of Public Prosecutions File relating to
    Tilley, Moody, Virgo, Alton, Brown et al, National Archives, released May 2013
The resources of the Pat Finucane Centre: www.patfinucanecentre.org
The Death of Samuel Devenny, Northern Ireland; Police Ombudsman's Report
    2001

Books

Campbell, Duncan: *That Was Business, This Is Personal*, Martin Secker &
    Warburg, London 1990
Campbell, Duncan: *The Underworld*, BBC Books, London 1994
Cox, Barry; Shirley, John; Short, Martin: *The Fall of Scotland Yard*, Penguin,
    London 1977
Frost, George 'Jack': *Flying Squad*, Youth Book Club Ltd, London 1950

Glinert, Ed: *West End Chronicles*, Allen Lane, London 2007

Green, Shirley: *Rachman*, Michael Joseph, London 1979

Hambrook, Walter: *Hambrook of the Yard: The Memoirs of Ex-Detective Superintendent Walter Hambrook CID*, Robert Hale, London 1937

Hill, Billy (ghost. Duncan Webb): *Boss of Britain's Underworld*, Naldrett Press, London 1955

Kennedy, Ludovic (ed.): *Wicked Beyond Belief: The Luton Murder Case*, Granada Publishing, London 1980

Kennedy, Ludovic: *Thirty-Six Murders & Two Immoral Earnings*, Profile Books, London 2002

Kirby, Dick: *The Sweeney: The First Sixty Years of Scotland Yard's Crimebusting Flying Squad 1919–78*, Wharncliffe, Barnsely 2011

McNee, Sir David: *McNee's Law: The Memoirs of Sir David McNee*, William Collins Sons & Co. Ltd, London 1983

Mark, Sir Robert: *In the Office of Constable: An Autobiography*, William Collins Sons & Co. Ltd, London 1978

Morton, James: *Bent Coppers*, Little, Brown, London 1993

Morton, James: *Gangland Soho*, Piatkus, London 2008

Parker, Tony: *The Plough Boy*, Hutchinson, London 1965

Parris, John: *Scapegoat*, Duckworth, London 1991

Pyle, Joey: *Notorious: The Changing Face of Organised Crime*, Virgin Books, London 2005

Read, Leonard & Morton, James: *Nipper*, MacDonald, London 1991

Reynolds, Bruce: *The Autobiography of a Thief*, Virgin Books, London 2005

Sharpe, F.D: *Sharpe of the Flying Squad*, John Long, London 1938

Short, Martin: *Lundy: The Destruction of Scotland Yard's Finest Detective*, Grafton Books, London 1991

Sinclair, Iain: *London: City of Disappearances*, Penguin, London 2007

Smith, Terry: *Blaggers Inc.*, John Blake, 2012

Sparks, Ruby (with Norman Price): *Burglar to the Nobility*, Arthur Barker, London 1961

Thomas, Donald: *An Underworld at War*, John Murray, London 2003

Thomas, Donald: *Villains' Paradise*, John Murray, London 2005

Wickstead, *Commander Bert: Gangbuster*, Futura, London 1985

Newspapers and Magazines

Daily Mirror: Monday 6–Thursday 9 March 1972; Tuesday 30 March 1976; Wednesday 31 March, 1976; 'Portrait of the Sweeney Villain', Friday 8 July, 1977

News of the World: 'My Friends in the Underworld', 21 May 1972; 'Yard Chief Sensation', 28 May 1972; 'Vice Boom: Shock Disclosures', 4 June, 1972

Penthouse Magazine, Vol. 8 No.6, 'The Sutton Report, 1973'

Sunday People: 'Police Chief and the "Porn" King', by Laurie Manifold, 27 February 1972; 'Another Indiscreet Holiday', by Laurie Manifold, 5 March 1972

The Sun: 'Shouts at Top Ex-Yard Man in the Dock', Wednesday 31 March 1976; 'Downfall of the Man who Led the Sweeney', Thursday 7 July 1977; Friday 8 July 1977; 'Porn Chief who Aided Yard Set to Go Free', Monday 11 July 1977

The Times: 'Obituary: Jeremiah Lynch', 15 July 1953

Radio And Television Transcripts

The following interviews given by Kenneth Drury:

ITN News at Ten, 7 March 1972
PM Reports, 7 March 1972
BBC2 News, 9 March 1972
BBC TV News, 5.50 p.m., 9 March 1972
BBC World at One, 9 March 1972

Interview

With Ex-Metropolitan Police Inspector Andrew Gorzynski, 31 January 2013. (Thank you to Mr Gorzynski for his valuable insights into the Metropolitan Police in the late 1970s.)

INDEX